A Simple French Grammar

With Exercises

Susan A. Girelli, M.A., A.I.L.
Chesham High School

Hodder & Stoughton

A MEMBER OF THE HODDER HEADLINE GROUP

D0228450

Orders: please contact Bookpoint Ltd, 39 Milton Park, Abingdon, Oxon
OX14 4TD. Telephone: (44) 01235 400414, Fax: (44) 01235 400454.
Lines are open from 9.00-6.00, Monday to Saturday, with a 24 hour message
answering service. Email address: orders@bookpoint.co.uk

British Library Cataloguing in Publication Data
Girelli, Susan
   A Simple French Grammar.
   1. French language – Grammar – 1951 –
   I. Title
   448'2'421   PC2112

ISBN 0 7131 0324 8

First published 1979
Impression number   21 20 19 18 17 16 15
Year   2005 2004 2003 2002 2001 2000 1999

Printed in Great Britain for Hodder & Stoughton Educational,
a division of Hodder Headline Plc, 338 Euston Road, London NW1 3BH
by Athenæum Press Ltd, Gateshead, Tyne & Wear.

Preface

This book is intended to be used by average pupils and pupils of moderate ability, whose knowledge of English grammar is too limited to enable them to use, with ease, any of the excellent advanced French grammars already available.

It is intended as a handy reference book for homework and exam revision, and as a companion to the major basic courses.

The contents aim to cover basic grammar points up to first examinations in simple terms. Grammarians will no doubt notice omissions and superficial explanations, but I have only dealt with points I feel can be handled by pupils of average ability, and which will be practical and relevant.

My thanks to Peter I. Hill for his patience and encouragement, and to my parents Mr. & Mrs. D. Edmunds for their helpful enthusiasm.

S.G.

This book is dedicated to the foundation year pupils of Frogmore Comprehensive School, Yateley, Hants, 1975.

Abbreviations

cont.	continued		*masc.*	masculine
e.g.	for example		*N.B.*	note carefully
etc.	and so on		*s.*	singular
f.	feminine		*sing.*	singular
fem.	feminine		*pl.*	plural
m.	masculine			

Contents

6 *Contents*

Explanation of English terms used

Adjective

An adjective is a word that describes, or tells you something about a person, place, animal or thing. **Big, pretty, tall, young** and all the colours are adjectives.

Adverb

An adverb tells you something about a verb, or action word. It can tell you *how* a thing is done, e.g. **quickly, well, happily.** It can tell you *when* an action is done, e.g. **often, always, usually.**

Apostrophe

This is a comma 'in the air' which shows you that a letter is missing. **He's** should really be **he is** and the apostrophe shows that the i is missing.

Consonant

Consonants are all the letters of the alphabet, except the letters A, E, I, O, U, Y.

Infinitive

This is the part of the verb that does not mention any person, but has to in front of it. **To make, to swim, to fall** are all infinitives.

Noun

A noun is a person, place, animal or thing, e.g., **John, a girl, the beach, the dog.**

Negative

A negative often shows that something is *not* to be done. **Not, never, no more** are all negatives.

Object

The object of a verb is the noun or pronoun that the verb *acts on*, and that is mentioned after the verb, e.g.:

We sold the car. **Car** is the object.
I saw them. **Them** is the object.

There can be a *direct object* and an *indirect object*. The above examples are direct objects. An indirect object usually has the word **to** before the noun or pronoun. To find out which is the indirect object, try to put *to* before the nouns/pronouns that come after the verb. The one that makes most sense is the indirect object, and the remaining one (if any) is the direct object, e.g., I gave **him the present.** If you changed the order slightly you could put *to* in front of **him** (I gave the present to **him**), but it would not make sense if you put *to* in front of **the present.** So the indirect object is **him** and the direct object is **the present.**

The Passive

The passive shows what *was done* to someone, rather than the action someone *did*, e.g.:

He was wounded. **Was wounded** is a passive verb.
They have been invited. **Have been invited** is a passive verb.

Past participle

The past participle of a verb is the part that usually goes with *has* and *have*. It shows that the action has taken place in the past. It often ends in ed but there are many exceptions.

You have walked. **Walked** is the past participle.
He has thrown. **Thrown** is the past participle.

Plural

This means that there is more than one noun mentioned. There is usually an s at the end of the noun, e.g., some cats, the ladies.

Possessive adjective

A possessive adjective shows who a person, place, animal, or thing belongs to, e.g., **his** son, **your** horse, **my** book.

Possessive pronoun

A possessive pronoun shows who a person, place, animal, or thing belongs to, but this time the person, place, etc., does not follow the possessive word, or is not mentioned at all, e.g.:

That dress is **hers**. This is **mine**.

Preposition

A word, often indicating position, which comes before a noun or pronoun, e.g., **at** the station, **to** the city, **with** my friend, **against** the wall.

Pronoun

A pronoun takes the place of a noun. Instead of repeating the name **John** all the time, you could use **he**. If you use a pronoun before a verb (as a subject), use the forms:

I, you, he, she, it, we, they.

If you put a pronoun after a verb (as an object), use the forms:

me, you, him, her, it, us, them.

For example, **Michael** likes **animals.**
He likes **them.**

Reflexive verbs

These verbs do not exist in English in the same way as they do in French. Reflexive verbs show that someone is doing something *to himself*, e.g.:

He shot **himself.** I scratched **myself.**

In English the verbs have a meaning without **himself, myself** etc. With French reflexive verbs, the French word for **myself, yourself,** etc., must always be there, even though it may have no separate meaning in English. (*See Chapters 18 & 19*)

Relative pronouns

Relative pronouns are the words **who, whom, which,** and **that,** which link sentences, e.g.:

She is the girl **who** bought my bike.
I found the pen **that** I had lost.

Often in English, **that** is used instead of all the other forms, or no word may be used at all, e.g.:

There's the book I want.
There's the book **that** I want.

Singular

Only one noun is mentioned, e.g., **a pig, the spade, a boy.**

Subject

The subject of a verb (or sentence) is the noun or pronoun which comes before the verb, and which does the action, e.g.:

John works hard. **John** is the subject.
She is knitting. **She** is the subject.

Tense

Tense indicates the different times when actions take place, e.g., present, future, past. Tense describes the time of the verb, and verbs have different forms for each tense, e.g.:

Present　I have
Future　　I shall have
Past　　　I had

Explanations of individual tenses are given in the text.

Verb

A verb is a doing or being word which describes an action or a state: I **like**, he **works**, she **is.**

Vowel

Vowels are the letters **A, E, I, O, U.** The letters H and Y can sometimes be used as vowels.

A Simple French Grammar

1) Un, une = a, an

Every *noun* in French is either *masculine* or *feminine*, even things like books and chairs. To show masculine words you use **un**, e.g.:

un stylo, un livre.

To show feminine words you use **une**, e.g.:

une chaise, une table.

Exercise

Put **un** or **une** in front of these words:

a) règle b) livre c) chien d) gomme e) fille

2) Le, la, l' and les = the

There are four ways to say *the* in French. Three are singular, and one is for all plural words.

Le: for most masculine words that are singular, e.g.:
le chat, le garçon.
La: for most feminine words that are singular, e.g.:
la vache, la femme.
L': for singular words that begin in French with *a, e, i, o, u* and sometimes *h*, e.g.:
l'école, l'huile.
Les: for all plural words. This time it does not matter if the words are masculine or feminine, e.g.:
les chiens, les filles.

Exercise

Put in **le, la, l'** or **les** in front of these words:

a) cahiers b) encre c) chaise d) fenêtres e) pupitre f) maison
g) pomme h) jardin i) ballon j) hôtel

3) Cardinal numbers 1 to 1000

1	un, une	71	soixante et onze
2	deux	72	soixante-douze
3	trois	73	soixante-treize
4	quatre	74	soixante-quatorze
5	cinq	75	soixante-quinze
6	six	76	soixante-seize
7	sept	77	soixante-dix-sept
8	huit	78	soixante-dix-huit
9	neuf	79	soixante-dix-neuf
10	dix	80	quatre-vingts
11	onze	81	quatre-vingt-un
12	douze	82	quatre-vingt-deux
13	treize	83	quatre-vingt-trois
14	quatorze	84	quatre-vingt-quatre
15	quinze	85	quatre-vingt-cinq
16	seize	86	quatre-vingt-six
17	dix-sept	87	quatre-vingt-sept
18	dix-huit	88	quatre-vingt-huit
19	dix-neuf	89	quatre-vingt-neuf
20	vingt	90	quatre-vingt-dix
21	vingt et un	91	quatre-vingt-onze
22	vingt-deux	92	quatre-vingt-douze
30	trente	93	quatre-vingt-treize
31	trente et un	94	quatre-vingt-quatorze
32	trente-deux	95	quatre-vingt-quinze
40	quarante	96	quatre-vingt-seize
41	quarante et un	97	quatre-vingt-dix-sept
42	quarante-deux	98	quatre-vingt-dix-huit
50	cinquante	99	quatre-vingt-dix-neuf
51	cinquante et un	100	cent
52	cinquante-deux	101	cent un
60	soixante	200	deux cents
61	soixante et un	500	cinq cents
62	soixante-deux	850	huit cents cinquante
70	soixante-dix	1000	mille

The numbers not found here can be formed as in English, e.g., **35** = **trente-cinq**, 48 = **quarante-huit**, and so on. Special uses of numbers will be found under separate sections, e.g., dates.

Exercise

Write out these numbers as French words.

a) twenty-six b) thirty-four c) forty-nine d) fifty-seven
e) sixty-five

4) Ordinal numbers – first, second, third, etc.

To form these numbers, in most cases add **ième** to the usual number,
e.g.:

> **huit** = eight, **huitième** = eighth

The exception to this is *first*, which is **premier** (or **première**, in the
feminine). However, for *twenty-first*, *thirty-first*, etc., you should
follow the usual rule, e.g.:

> **vingt et un** = twenty-one, **vingt et unième** = twenty-first

Remember to use these numbers like adjectives (*See Chapter 23*),
e.g.:

> **Le premier** jour de ma vie. = **The first** day of my life.

> Elle est **la troisième** femme de Claude. = She is Claude's **third**
> wife.

> Les **trois premières** filles. = The **first three** girls.

Note the word order in this special phrase.

Exercise

Write out these numbers as French words.

a) sixth b) eleventh c) thirty-seventh d) eighty-second e) fifty-first

5) Days of the week, months of the year

Days

Monday	lundi	Friday	vendredi
Tuesday	mardi	Saturday	samedi
Wednesday	mercredi	Sunday	dimanche
Thursday	jeudi		

Months

January	janvier	July	juillet
February	février	August	août
March	mars	September	septembre
April	avril	October	octobre
May	mai	November	novembre
June	juin	December	décembre

Note that capital letters are not used with the days and months in French.

Special points

a) No word for *on* is normally needed in French with the days of the week, e.g.:

I shall arrive on Monday evening. = J'arriverai **lundi soir.**

b) Le in front of a day gives the idea of *every*, e.g.:

I go to market **on Saturdays.** = Je vais au marché **le samedi.**
Le jeudi = On Thursdays = every Thursday

c) **En,** or **au mois de** mean *in* with months. Either expression may be used, e.g.:

He will go to Paris **in October.** = Il ira à Paris } **en octobre**
au mois d'octobre

Exercise

Put into French the following:

a) on Wednesday b) on Saturdays c) on Monday morning
d) in March e) in December

6) **Dates**

The normal numbers 2—31 are used with dates and no word for *of* is needed, e.g.:

The **12th** (of) May = Le **douze** mai
The **16th** (of) August = Le **seize** août

The first of the month is a special case. Use **premier.**

The 1st (of) June = Le **premier** juin
The 1st (of) March = Le **premier** mars

En is used with years to mean in, e.g.:

> In 1980 = En dix-neuf cent quatre-vingt (en 1980)
> In 1856 = En dix-huit cent cinquante-six (en 1856)

Exercise

Write the following out as French words:

a) 19th August b) 1st May c) 26th June d) in 1982 e) in 1066

7) Time

To tell the time in French, you must know the numbers 1—29, and you must remember to *put the hour first and then the minutes.*

It is **two o'clock** = Il est **deux heures**
It is **quarter past** two = Il est deux heures **et quart**
It is **half past** two = Il est deux heures **et demie**
It is **quarter to** three = Il est trois heures **moins le quart**
It is **ten past** three = Il est trois heures **dix**
It is **five to** four = Il est quatre heures **moins cinq**

Special points

a) Do not use the number **douze** for twelve o'clock:

> It is twelve o'clock (**noon**) = Il est **midi**
> It is twelve o'clock (**midnight**) = Il est **minuit**

b) Note the spelling of **demi** when used with **midi** and **minuit** only.

> It is **half past twelve** (day) = Il est **midi et demi**
> It is **half past twelve** (night) = Il est **minuit et demi**

c) It is **one o'clock** = Il est **une heure** (*note no s*)

d) The following chart may help you to remember the words you use for minutes and parts of hours.

[Il est neuf heures]	et quart = quarter past et demie = half past moins le quart = quarter to cinq = five past vingt = twenty past moins quatre = four minutes to moins vingt-cinq = twenty-five to	*no word* *for past* *needed*

e) At = A, e.g.:

He will arrive at half past seven. = Il arrivera à sept heures et demie.
I leave school at four o'clock. = Je quitte l'école à quatre heures.

Exercise

Put the following into French:

a) It is eight o'clock b) It is half past ten c) It is noon
d) It is quarter to six e) It is twenty-five past seven

8) Weather and Seasons

All the seasons in French are *masculine*: l'été, l'automne, l'hiver, le printemps. Certain prepositions are generally used with them:

en été = in summer
en automne = in autumn
en hiver = in winter
au printemps = in spring

Here are some common descriptions of the weather:

Il **fait beau.** = It is fine.
Il **fait mauvais.** = It is not fine.
Il **fait chaud.** = It is hot (warm).
Il **fait froid.** = It is cold.
Il **fait frais.** = It is cool.
Il **fait du soleil.** = It is sunny.
Il **fait du vent.** = It is windy.
Il **fait du brouillard.** = It is foggy.
Il **fait de l'orage.** = It is stormy.
Il **fait du tonnerre.** = It is thundering.
Il **pleut.** = It is raining.
Il **neige.** = It is snowing.
Il **gèle.** = It is freezing.
Il **grêle.** = It is hailing.
Un **orage.** = A storm.

To make the above expressions in the *past* tense, use il **faisait** instead of il **fait**, e.g.:

Il **faisait du vent** hier soir. = It **was windy** yesterday evening.

In the same way, **il pleut** becomes **il pleuvait,** e.g.:

Il pleuvait ce matin. = **It was raining** this morning.

Il neige becomes il neigeait, e.g.:

Il neigeait hier. = **It was snowing** yesterday.

Il gèle and **il grêle** become **il gelait** and **il grêlait.**

Remember the useful expressions:

Par un beau jour d'été . . . = **On** a fine summer's day . . .
Par un mauvais soir d'hiver . . . = **On** a miserable winter's
evening . . .

Exercise

Write down two types of weather to describe each season, e.g.:

En été, il fait chaud.

9) Some/any

	singular	*plural*
masculine	**du**	**des**
feminine	**de la**	**des**
before a vowel or h	**de l'**	**des**

There is *one* plural form: **des.** The others are all singular. With masculine singular words like **sucre** (sugar), **thé** (tea), use **du,** e.g.:

some sugar – **du** sucre
some tea = **du** thé

With feminine singular words like **farine** (flour), **viande** (meat), use **de la,** e.g.:

some flour = **de la** farine
some meat = **de la** viande

With *singular* words beginning with *a, e, i, o, u* and sometimes *h*, in French, like **eau** (water), **huile** (oil), use **de l'**, e.g.:

some water = **de l'**eau
some oil = **de l'**huile

With *all* plural words like **livres** (books), **œufs** (eggs), use **des**, e.g.:

> some books = **des** livres
> some eggs = **des** œufs

So far, we have only mentioned *some*. In English, *any* is used instead of some in a question and after not. (Have you **any** flour? No, I haven't **any** flour.) In *questions* in French, you can use the same forms given in the chart at the beginning of this section, e.g.:

> Have you **any** butter? = Avez-vous **du** beurre?
> Are there **any** oranges? = Est-ce qu'il y a **des** oranges?

However, you must use **de** (or **d'** before a vowel or h) instead of du, de la, de l', or des *after not*. In French not = **ne** . . . verb . . . **pas**. For example:

> Are there **any** red pens? = Est-ce qu'il y a **des** stylos rouges?
> No, there aren't any red pens. = Non, il **n'y a pas de** stylos rouges.
> Have you **any** ink? = Avez-vous **de** l'encre?
> No, I **haven't any** ink. = Non, je **n'ai pas d'**encre.

De is also used after **ne** . . . verb . . . **plus** = no more, and **ne** . . . verb . . . **jamais** = never. (See Chapter 17)

Special point

De is used when a noun in the plural follows its adjective, e.g., some fine trees = **de beaux arbres.**

Exercise

Fill in the correct form of some — **du, de la, de l'** or **des.**

a) J'ai . . . stylos.
b) Il mange . . . fromage.
c) Est-ce qu'il y a . . . encre sur le pupitre?
d) Nous préparons . . . soupe.
e) Elle achète . . . croissants.

10) Combinations of A and De

à + le = au		de + le = du	
à + la = à la	= to the,	de + la = de la	of the,
à + l' = à l'	at the	de + l' = de l'	= from the,
à + les = aux		de + les = des	some

These forms can be used for any of the above meanings when necessary.

Examples

Elle donne une pomme **au** professeur. = She gives an apple **to the** teacher.
Je suis à l'école. = I am at (the) school.
Il offre des oranges **aux** garçons. = He offers some oranges **to the** boys.
Elle est la mère **de la** jeune fille. = She is the mother **of the** girl.
Nous rentrons **du** village. = We are returning **from the** village.

The above forms are not used with names of people or places. Use à or **de** alone.

Examples

Il arrive **de** Nice. = He is arriving **from** Nice.
Elle est la sœur **de** Pierre. = She is the sister **of** Pierre.
Nous allons à Paris. = We are going to Paris.
Il donne un cadeau à Claudine. = He gives a present to Claudine.

Exercises

Put **au, à la, à l'**, or **aux** in front of the following:

a) café b) cinéma c) champs d) épicerie e) gare

Put **du, de la, de l'**, or **des** in front of the following:

a) bois b) école c) facteur d) magasins e) rivière

11) **De of possession**

In English we can use *'s* or *s'* to show possession, e.g.: *John's* book, *the boys'* father. In French you *must* turn it back to front and use **de** = of, e.g.:

It's **John's** book. = C'est le livre **de** Jean. (It's the book **of John**.)

Mr Brown is **Susan's** father. = M. Lebrun est le père **de** Suzanne. (Mr Brown is the father **of Susan**.)

If you do not *name* the person, you must use **de** + **le, la, l'** or **les**. (See previous chapter.) For example:

Mrs Maurois is the children's mother. = Mme. Maurois est la mère des enfants. (Mrs Maurois is the mother of the children.) It's the boy's bicycle. = C'est le vélo du garçon. (It's the bicycle of the boy.)

Exercise

Fill in **de, d'** or a combination of **de** (See Chapter 10):

a) C'est la voiture . . . professeur.
b) Voici la règle . . . Michel.
c) Il porte le pantalon . . . Alain.
d) Je cherche le sac . . . marchande.
e) Nous voyons la camionnette . . . épicier.

12) Subject pronouns – I, you, he, she, it, we, they

je	= I	nous	= we
tu	= you	vous	= you
il	= he, it	ils	= they
elle	= she, it	elles	= they

Subject pronouns take the place of nouns which are the subject of a verb and show who is doing the action. There is another subject pronoun, not listed above, which is commonly used in spoken French: **on**. This pronoun is discussed fully in Chapter 44.

There are *two forms* for *you*, *it*, and *they*.

tu = you (*one person*) — used when talking to close friends or relatives
vous = you — used when talking to *several people or to one person you do not know well*
il = it — used for animals and things that are *masculine*. (e.g. le chat, le livre)
elle = it — used for animals and things that are *feminine* (e.g. la vache, la règle)
ils = they — used for masculine words and groups of men or boys, and mixed groups of masculine and feminine words and people
elles = they — used for feminine words and groups of girls and women

Examples

Le chat est dans le jardin. ⟶ Il est dans le jardin.
La serviette est sur le lit. ⟶ Elle est sur le lit.
Les cahiers sont sur la table. ⟶ Ils sont sur la table.
Les garçons sont dans la cour. ⟶ Ils sont dans la cour.
Paul et Claudine sont à la maison. ⟶ Ils sont à la maison.
Le stylo et la règle sont sur le livre. ⟶ Ils sont sur le livre.
Les chaises sont sur les tables. ⟶ Elles sont sur les tables.
Claudine et Marie sont en ville. ⟶ Elles sont en ville.

13) Er verbs

a) *Present tense*
To be able to use a verb in French, you must know the *infinitive*,
that is, the part that mentions no person but has *to* before it in
English, e.g., to do, to eat, to wash, etc. The infinitive of this group
of verbs in French always ends in er — hence the name. The next
step is to find the *stem* by taking off the er at the end of the
infinitive, e.g.:

chanter = to sing   stem = chant
donner = to give   stem = donn

To the *stem*, you must add one of the endings given in the chart
below. Don't forget to put in the French for 'I, we, you,' etc. at
the beginning. (See Chapter 12)

ER verb endings

je has ending e	nous has ending ons
tu has ending es	vous has ending ez
il has ending e	ils has ending ent
elle has ending e	elles has ending ent

Examples

a) We like ⟶ to like = aimer ⟶ stem = aim.
We = nous and has ending ons. Add ons to the stem (aim).
Final answer: Nous aimons.
b) She prepares ⟶ to prepare = préparer ⟶ stem = prépar.
She = elle and has ending e. Add e to the stem (prépar).
Final answer: Elle prépare.

Special point

If the words *am, is, are* are followed by a word ending in *ing* in
English, (e.g., he is eating), you must ignore *am, is, are* in French.

Use only the word ending in *ing*. As far as French is concerned, *he is eating* is exactly the same as *he eats*. So both these sentences in French must be Il **mange**.

Example

We are playing. Ignore are ⟶ to play = jouer ⟶ stem = jou. We = nous and has ending ons. Add ons to the stem (jou). Final answer: **Nous jouons.**

Exercise

Fill in the correct form of the verb given in brackets.

a) Je . . . la télévision. (regarder)
b) Ils . . . au football. (jouer)
c) Nous . . . le chien. (chercher)
d) Tu . . . une glace. (manger)
e) Vous . . . trop vite! (marcher)

b) *Commands: er verbs*
To make a command (e.g., Stand up!; Eat your lunch!; Be quiet!), with an er verb, find the stem and then add e if you are talking to a person you know well, or add ez if you are talking to a person you do not know well, or to several people.

Examples

Mange ta glace, maman! = Eat your ice-cream, Mum!
Regardez cette voiture, monsieur! = Look at that car, sir!
Cherchez le chien, mes enfants! = Look for the dog, children!

Use **ne** . . . **pas** if you want to tell someone *not* to do something. **Ne** and **pas** go on either side of the verb. (See Chapter 17) For example:

Ne mange pas si vite, Pierre! = Don't eat so quickly, Peter!

c) *Let's: er verbs*
Let's go for a walk. Let's buy some fruit.
To make this kind of suggestion with an er verb, find the stem and add **ons**. No other word is needed for *let's*.

Examples

Jouons au football. = **Let's** play football.

Préparons du thé. = **Let's** prepare some tea.
Ne regardons pas la télévision. = **Let's not** watch television.
Note that ne . . . pas can be used in the same way as with commands. (see Chapter 13b)

Exercise

Put the correct *command* in a), b), c) and the correct *let's* form in d) and e). The verbs to use are given in brackets.

a) . . . le sucre, s'il vous plaît, monsieur. (passer)
b) Ne . . . pas le chien, Pierre. (chasser)
c) . . . les fenêtres, les garçons. (fermer)
d) . . . au tennis. (jouer)
e) . . . dans le cinéma. (entrer)

14) Ir verbs

a) *Present tense*
Find the stem by removing **ir** from the infinitive. Then add one of the endings given below, just as you did with er verbs. (See Chapter 13a)

IR verb endings

je has ending is	**nous** has ending issons
tu has ending is	**vous** has ending issez
il has ending it	**ils** has ending issent
elle has ending it	**elles** has ending issent

Examples

a) They (m) choose ⟶ to choose = **choisir** ⟶ stem = **chois**.
They (m) = **ils** and has ending **issent**. Add issent to the stem
(**chois**). Final answer: **Ils choisissent.**
b) You (pl) fill ⟶ to fill = **remplir** ⟶ stem = **rempl**.
You (pl) = **vous** and has ending **issez**. Add issez to the stem
(**rempl**). Final answer: **Vous remplissez.**

Exercise

Fill in the correct form of the verb given in brackets.

a) Elle . . . un cadeau. (choisir)

b) Nous . . . les boîtes. (remplir)
c) Paul . . . le fromage. (finir)
d) Vous . . . la nappe. (salir)
e) Le général . . . le soldat. (punir)

b) *Commands: ir verbs*
To make a command with an ir verb, find the stem, and then add
is if you are talking to a person you know well, or add issez if you
are talking to a person you do not know well, or to several people,
for example:

Finis tes devoirs, Michel. = Finish your homework, Michael.
Choisissez un cadeau, madame. = Choose a gift, madam.

c) *Let's: ir verbs*
To form *let's* with an ir verb, find the stem, and then add issons:

Finissons le gâteau. = Let's finish the cake.
Choisissons des bonbons. = Let's choose some sweets.

Exercise

Put the correct *command* form in a), b), c) and the correct *let's*
form in d) and e). The verbs to use are given in brackets.

a) . . . l'exercice, les enfants. (finir)
b) Ne . . . pas la page, Alain. (salir)
c) . . . les verres, s'il vous plaît. (remplir)
d) . . . des cartes de Noël. (choisir)
e) Ne . . . pas les devoirs. (finir)

15) Re verbs

a) *Present tense*
Find the stem by removing re from the infinitive. Then add one of
the endings given below, just as you did with er and ir verbs. (See
Chapters 13a and 14a)

RE verb endings

je has ending s	nous has ending ons
tu has ending s	vous has ending ez
il has no ending	ils has ending ent
elle has no ending	elles has ending ent

NB il and elle have no endings. Use only the stem.

Examples

a) He sells ⟶ to sell = vendre ⟶ stem = vend.
He = il and has no ending. Use stem only (vend).
Final answer: Il vend.
b) I reply ⟶ to reply = répondre ⟶ stem = répond.
I = je and has ending s. Add s to the stem (répond).
Final answer: Je réponds.

Exercise

Fill in the correct form of the verb given in brackets.

a) Les petites filles . . . Hélène au coin de la rue. (attendre)
b) Est-ce que tu . . . la musique? (entendre)
c) Il . . . l'escalier. (descendre)
d) Nous . . . notre voiture. (vendre)
e) Vous . . . les clefs trop souvent. (perdre)

b) *Commands: re verbs*
To make a command with an re verb, find the stem, and then add
s if you are talking to a person you know well, or add ez if you are
talking to a person you do not know well, or to several people. For
example:

Vends ta voiture, papa. = Sell your car, dad.
Répondez aux questions, monsieur. = Answer the questions, sir.

c) *Let's: re verbs*
To form *let's* with an re verb, find the stem, and then add **ons**:

Rendons l'argent. = **Let's** give back the money.
Attendons ici. = **Let's** wait here.

Exercise

Put the correct *command* form in a), b), c) and the correct *let's*
form in d) and e). The verbs to use are given in brackets.

a) . . . à la question, Michel. (répondre)
b) . . . les livres, maintenant. (rendre)
c) . . . l'autobus là-bas. (attendre)
d) . . . du train ici. (descendre)
e) . . . la maison. (vendre)

16) Etre and avoir

a) *Present tense*
Etre and avoir are both very irregular in the present tense:

Etre = To Be

je suis = I am	nous sommes = we are
tu es = you (s) are	vous êtes = you (pl) are
il est = he, it is	ils sont = they (m) are
elle est = she, it is	elles sont = they (f) are

Avoir = To Have

j'ai = I have	nous avons = we have
tu as = you (s) have	vous avez = you (pl) have
il a = he, it has	ils ont = they (m) have
elle a = she, it has	elles ont = they (f) have

Exercise

Fill in the correct part of être or avoir.

a) J' . . . un chien.
b) Marianne . . . dans le salon.
c) Les enfants . . . beaucoup de devoirs.
d) Nous . . . dans la cuisine.
e) Tu . . . une grande voiture.

b) *Commands: être and avoir*
Commands with these two verbs are rarely used and are again
irregular:

Etre = To Be

Use **sois** if you are talking to a person you know well. Use **soyez**
if you are talking to a person you do not know well, or to several
people.

Avoir = To Have

Use **aie** if you are talking to a person you know well. Use **ayez** if
you are talking to a person you do not know well, or to several
people.

c) *Let's: être and avoir*
Again irregular in form and rarely used.

Etre = To Be
Soyons = Let's be

Avoir = To Have
Ayons = Let's have

17) Negatives

not, never, no-one, no more, no longer, nothing, neither . . . nor

a) *General use*
Negatives in French are placed on either side of the verb.

a) Ne . . . verb . . . pas = not.
Je ne veux pas y aller = I do not want to go (there).
b) Ne . . . verb . . . jamais = never or not ever.
Il ne fait jamais ses devoirs. = He never does his homework.
Elle n'arrive jamais à l'heure. = She doesn't ever arrive on time.
c) Ne . . . verb . . . personne = no-one, nobody, or not . . . anyone.
Il n'y a personne à la maison. = There is no-one, (nobody) at home.
Elle n'aime personne. = She doesn't like anyone.
d) Ne . . . verb . . . plus = no more, not . . . any more, no longer, or not . . . any longer.
Je n'ai plus d'argent. = I haven't any more money, *or* I have no more money.
Elle ne va plus à l'école. = She doesn't go to school any longer, *or*, she no longer goes to school.
e) Ne . . . verb . . . rien = nothing, or not . . . anything.
Nous n'avons rien à manger. = We have nothing to eat.
Il n'aime rien. = He doesn't like anything.
f) Ne . . . verb . . . ni . . . ni = neither . . . nor.
Il n'a ni sœurs ni frères. = He has neither sisters nor brothers.

b) *Jamais, personne, and rien, standing alone*
Jamais, personne, and rien, may stand alone as answers to questions.

Examples

Qui as-tu vu? — Personne. = Who did you see? — No-one.
Qu'est-ce que tu fais? — Rien. = What are you doing? — Nothing.
Vous avez déjà visité Paris? — Non, jamais. = Have you already visited Paris? — No, never.

c) *Personne and rien, at the beginning of a sentence*
Personne and **rien** may stand at the beginning of a sentence, with
ne following:

> **Personne** n'arrive. = **No-one** is coming.
> **Rien** n'est plus facile. = **Nothing** is easier.

Special points

When using any of the above negatives with the *perfect* or *past
perfect* tenses, (See Chapters 37, 39 & 42), **ne** is placed *before* the
part of avoir or être and **pas, rien**, etc., are placed *after* avoir or
être and *before* the past participle. There is one exception --
personne is always placed *after* the past participle.

Examples

> Je **n'ai jamais** vu Paris. = I have never seen Paris.
> Il **n'est pas** arrivé. = He did not arrive.
> Ils **n'avaient rien** mangé. = They had not eaten anything.
> Nous **n'avons** rencontré **personne**. = We did not meet anyone.

If you are asked a question containing any of the above negatives,
and you want to answer *yes*, you must use **si** (*not oui*).

> Tu **n'as** vu **personne**? = Didn't you see anyone?
> **Si**, j'ai vu quelqu'un. = Yes, I saw someone.

If you use any of the above negatives, remember that *un, une, du,
de la, de l'* and *des* must be replaced by **de**.

Examples

> Il a **une** chemise propre. = He has a clean shirt.
> Il n'a pas **de** chemise propre. = He hasn't a clean shirt.
> Je veux **du** chocolat. = I want some chocolate.
> Je ne veux pas **de** chocolat. = I do not want any chocolate.

Exercise

Put the *negatives* given in brackets in the correct place in the
sentence. Make any other necessary changes.

a) Pierre mange le fromage. (**ne** . . . **jamais**)
b) Nous voyons. (**ne** . . . **rien**)
c) Elle achète des bananes. (**ne** . . . **pas**)
d) Je vais au cinéma. (**ne** . . . **jamais**)

18) Reflexive pronouns

je	⟶ me		nous	⟶ nous
tu	⟶ te		vous	⟶ vous
il	⟶ se		ils	⟶ se
elle	⟶ se		elles	⟶ se

Reflexive pronouns are used with reflexive verbs (See Chapter 19). Reflexive verbs in French would be incomplete without the above pronouns. They can also be used to give the idea of *myself, yourself* etc., and *one another* or *each other*.

Examples

a) Reflexive verb: Il se rase. = He is shaving.
Tu te lèves. = You are getting up.
b) Other uses: Elle se regarde dans la glace. = She is looking at herself in the mirror.
Nous nous aimons. = We love each other.

19) Reflexive verbs

a) *Present tense*
Reflexive verbs can be found in any of the three groups of verbs (er, ir, re) and follow the same pattern, except that you must remember to use the reflexive pronoun (See Chapter 18), because otherwise it would not make sense in French. Most of the reflexive verbs you will meet will be er verbs. Here is an example:

Se coucher = To go to bed

je me couche	nous nous couchons
tu te couches	vous vous couchez
il se couche	ils se couchent
elle se couche	elles se couchent

Special point

If the infinitive of a reflexive verb is used along with another verb which is the main verb of the sentence, you must remember to change the *reflexive pronoun*, so that it matches the subject of the main verb:

Nous allons **nous** laver. = We are going to wash.

In the above example, the temptation would be to put *se* instead of the second **nous**, because you usually find *se* with the infinitive. However, the reflexive pronoun must match the subject, and in this case **nous** must be used.

Je n'aime pas **me** lever. = I don't like getting up.
(**me** to match **je**)
Elle va **se** reposer. = She is going to rest.
(**se** to match **elle**)

Exercise

Fill in the correct form of the verb given in brackets.

a) Je . . . dans ma chambre. (se reposer)
b) Pierre et André . . . dans le parc. (se promener)
c) Est-ce que vous . . . dans la rivière? (se baigner)
d) Annette . . . dans la salle de bains. (se laver)
e) Nous allons . . . de bonne heure, demain. (se lever)

b) *Commands: reflexive verbs*
Reflexive verbs require the correct ending as for other verbs, plus -**toi** if you are talking to a person you know well, or -**vous** if you are talking to a person you do not know well, or to several people. For example:

Réveille-**toi**, Hélène. = Wake up, Helen.
Dépêchez-**vous** les garçons,= Hurry up, boys.

If, however, you are telling someone *not* to do something, use the normal reflexive pronouns **te** or **vous** *before* the verb. For example:

Ne **te** lève pas. = Don't get up.
Ne **vous** peignez pas ici! = Don't comb your hair here!

c) *Let's: reflexive verbs*
Reflexive verbs require the correct ending as for other verbs, plus -**nous**:

Promenons-**nous**. = **Let's** go for a walk.
Dépêchons-**nous**. = **Let's** hurry.

If, however, you are making the suggestion *Let's not . . .*, use the reflexive pronoun **nous** before the verb as normal:

Ne nous couchons **pas** encore. = **Let's not** go to bed yet.
Ne nous reposons **pas.** = **Let's not** rest.

Exercise

Put the correct *command* form in a), b), c), and the correct *let's* form in d) and e). The verbs to use are given in brackets.

a) . . ., Pierre. (se réveiller)
b) . . . vite, les enfants. (s'habiller)
c) Ne . . . pas maintenant. (se coucher)
d) . . . près de la rivière. (se promener)
e) . . . d'aller aux magasins. (se dépêcher)

20) Question forms

a) Any statement can be made into a question by putting **Est-ce que** at the beginning of the sentence, or by putting **n'est-ce pas** at the end of the sentence. **Est-ce que** has *no* meaning in itself. **N'est-ce pas**, which is a more old-fashioned way of asking a question, can have several meanings, depending on the sentence, such as *won't you, should he, did we, haven't I* etc. **N'est-ce pas** is not as frequently used in spoken French as **Est-ce que**.

Statement	*Question*
Il y a des pommes. There are some apples.	a) Est-ce qu'il y a des pommes? Are there any apples? b) Il y a des pommes, **n'est-ce pas?** There are some apples, aren't there?

b) *Inversion* — to make a question by turning the subject and verb back to front, just as we do in English:

That is your brother.   Is that your brother?

Examples

Vous avez du thé.   Avez-vous du thé?
You have some tea.   Have you any tea?

Elle a un chien.   A-t-elle un chien?
She has a dog.   Has she a dog?

For the sake of the sound, you put a *t* between two vowels as in the above example. In most cases, it would be wrong to use this question form with **je**. Instead, you should use **est-ce que**:

Est-ce que je mange le fromage? = Do I eat cheese?

Exercise

Change the following sentences into questions, using **Est-ce que** or *inversion*.

a) Les couteaux sont sur la nappe.
b) Elles ont une belle maison.
c) Nous préparerons un bon dîner.
d) Tu fais tes devoirs.
e) Vous entendez la musique.

Reference list of question forms

Combien?	How much?
	How many?
Comment?	How?
	What . . . like? (asking for a description)
Est-ce que?	Has no real meaning but can turn any statement into a question.
Où?	Where?
Pourquoi?	Why?
Quand?	When?
Que, Qu'est-ce que?	What?
Qu'est-ce que c'est?	What is it?
Qu'est-ce qu'il y a?	What is (there)?
Qui?	Who?
Qui est-ce?	Who is it?

21) **Prepositions with names of towns and countries – at, to, in, from**

Names of Towns

a) *In, to, at* with the names of towns is à, e.g.: à Paris.

b) *Of, from* with the names of towns is de (d' before a vowel or h), e.g.: de Londres.

Names of Countries

a) *In, to* with *feminine* countries (the majority) is en, e.g.: en France, en Suisse. *In, to* with *masculine* countries is au, e.g.: au Japon, au Canada.
b) *From* with *feminine* countries is de (d' before a vowel or h), e.g.: Il vient de Suisse (d'Italie). *From* with *masculine* countries is du, e.g.: Je viens du Portugal.
c) *Of* with countries is usually de plus le, la, l'. (Remember de + le = du.) For example, les rivières de l'Allemagne. = The rivers of Germany; le nord de la France. = the north of France.

Special points

Some countries are plural, e.g.: les Etats-Unis = the United States. *In, to* with plural countries is aux, e.g.: Aux Etats-Unis. *From, of* with plural countries is des, e.g.: Il vient des Etats-Unis.

Exercise

Put in the correct form of the preposition used with the towns and countries named in the sentences.

a) Je viens . . . Canada.
b) M. Jauvert va souvent . . . Suisse.
c) Mon ami arrivera . . . Lyon demain.
d) Nous rentrons . . . Etats-Unis.
e) Est-ce que vous êtes . . . Londres?

Reference list of names of countries

Africa	L'Afrique	Holland	La Hollande
Australia	L'Australie	Ireland	L'Irlande
Austria	L'Autriche	Italy	L'Italie
Belgium	La Belgique	Russia	La Russie
Canada	Le Canada	Scotland	L'Ecosse
England	L'Angleterre	Spain	L'Espagne
Europe	L'Europe	Switzerland	La Suisse
France	La France	U.K.	Le Royaume-Uni
Germany	L'Allemagne	U.S.A.	Les Etats-Unis
Great Britain	La Grande Bretagne	Wales	Le Pays de Galles

22) Prepositions with means of transport

These expressions are best learned by heart.

By air	en avion	On horseback	à cheval
By bike	en vélo	By lorry	en camion
By boat	en bateau	By van	en camionnette
By bus	en autobus	By moped	en vélomoteur
By car	en voiture	By motorbike	en moto
By coach	en autocar	By taxi	en taxi
On foot	à pied	By train	par le train

Exercise

Put in the correct preposition used with the means of transport given in the sentences.

a) Nous allons à Paris . . . train.
b) Elle voyage . . . avion.
c) La famille va faire une promenade . . . voiture.
d) Les enfants vont en ville . . . pied.
e) Je vais rentrer . . . autobus.

23) Adjectives

Adjectives in French must be masculine or feminine, and singular or plural, to match the *noun* they are describing. You will probably learn adjectives in the masculine singular form, e.g.: **grand** = **big**, **jeune** = **young**. From the chart below, you can see that you should add certain letters in order to make the adjectives match their nouns.

masculine singular	=	add **nothing**
feminine singular	=	add **e** to masculine singular form
masculine plural	=	add **s** to masculine singular form
feminine plural	=	add **es** to masculine singular form

N.B. If an adjective ends in **e** already, like, **rouge** = red, *do not add another* e to make it feminine. Similarly, if an adjective ends in **s** already, like, **frais** = fresh, *do not add another* s to make it plural.

Examples

Masculine Singular	*Feminine Singular*
un **joli** chapeau	une **jolie** robe
un crayon **rouge**	une voiture **rouge**

Masculine Plural	*Feminine Plural*
de **jolis** chapeaux	de **jolies** robes
des crayons **rouges**	des voitures **rouges**

From the examples, you can see that some adjectives are placed before the noun, and some follow it. The general rule is that adjectives *follow* the noun they describe. Adjectives of *colour, shape* and *nationality* **must** follow. Adjectives of nationality do not usually have a capital letter. There are some common adjectives which may come before the noun. These are:

beau	=	beautiful	**joli**	=	pretty
bon	=	good	**long**	=	long
cher	=	dear	**mauvais**	=	bad
gentil	=	kind	**méchant**	=	naughty
grand	=	big	**meilleur**	=	better
gros	=	fat	**petit**	=	small
haut	=	high	**vieux**	=	old
jeune	=	young	**vilain**	=	wicked, naughty

Exercise

Fill in the correct form of the adjective given in brackets.

a) Elle porte une . . . jupe. (joli)
b) Nous mangeons de . . . glaces. (grand)
c) Chantal cherche un stylo . . . (noir)
d) Regardez les chiens . . . (brun)
e) Voilà de . . . champs. (petit)

24) Special adjectives

These adjectives do not follow the general rule, and have special spellings in their different forms. Here are the most common ones:

Masc. sing.	Fem. sing.	Masc. pl.	Fem. pl.	Meaning
beau	belle	beaux	belles	beautiful
blanc	blanche	blancs	blanches	white
bon	bonne	bons	bonnes	good
bref	brève	brefs	brèves	brief
cher	chère	chers	chères	dear
doux	douce	doux	douces	sweet
frais	fraîche	frais	fraîches	fresh, cool
gentil	gentille	gentils	gentilles	kind, gentle
heureux	heureuse	heureux	heureuses	happy
long	longue	longs	longues	long
neuf	neuve	neufs	neuves	new
nouveau	nouvelle	nouveaux	nouvelles	new
sec	sèche	secs	sèches	dry
vieux	vieille	vieux	vieilles	old

Special point

Beau, vieux, and **nouveau** have alternative masculine singular forms which should only be used with words beginning with a vowel or h. Feminine singular words beginning with a vowel or h, require the normal feminine singular form. Alternative masculine singular forms:

beau becomes **bel**
vieux becomes **vieil**
nouveau becomes **nouvel**

Examples

Un **bel** homme. = A handsome man.
Un **vieil** éléphant. = An old elephant.
Le **Nouvel** An. = The New Year.

Exercise

Fill in the correct form of the adjective given in brackets.

a) Il a une chemise . . . (blanc)
b) C'est un . . . fromage. (bon)
c) Maman achète des chaussures . . . (neuf)
d) Nous avons deux . . . voitures. (vieux)
e) Elles sont . . . (gentil)

25) Possessive adjectives – my, your, his, etc.

Since these are adjectives, they must match the word they describe, just like any other adjective. (See Chapter 23). Be careful *not* to match the possessive adjective with the person who is the owner, e.g.: She loves her dog. **Her**, in French, has to be matched with **dog**.

| | Singular | | Plural |
	Masculine	Feminine	
my	mon	ma	mes
your	ton	ta	tes
his	son	sa	ses
her	son	sa	ses
its	son	sa	ses
our	notre	notre	nos
your	votre	votre	vos
their	leur	leur	leurs

Note that there is only one plural form for each possessive.

Examples

It's my schoolbag. = C'est **mon** cartable.
She is our mother. = Elle est **notre** mère.
He is writing to his son. = Il écrit à **son** fils.
She is writing to her son. = Elle écrit à **son** fils.

Special points

a) You should avoid using the above possessive adjectives with names of parts of the body. (See Chapter 54)
b) Use the masculine singular form of the possessive adjective with feminine singular words that begin with a vowel or h. Masculine singular words that begin with a vowel or h use the normal masculine singular form of the possessive adjective, for example:

Mon amie est en vacances. = My friend (female) is on holiday.
Son armoire est plein de jouets. = His cupboard is full of toys.

Exercise

Fill in the correct form of the *possessive adjective* given in brackets.

a) Nous aimons . . . nouvelle maison. (our)
b) Les enfants enlèvent . . . veste. (their)
c) Je cherche . . . parapluie. (my)

d) Tu laves . . . robe. (your)
e) Vous quittez . . . bureau de bonne heure. (your)

26) Possessive pronouns – mine, yours, his, etc.

Possessive pronouns are used instead of possessive adjectives + noun. The same rules for matching apply. (See Chapter 25).

	Singular		Plural	
	Masculine	Feminine	Masculine	Feminine
mine	le mien	la mienne	les miens	les miennes
yours	le tien	la tienne	les tiens	les tiennes
his	le sien	la sienne	les siens	les siennes
hers	le sien	la sienne	les siens	les siennes
its	le sien	la sienne	les siens	les siennes
ours	le nôtre	la nôtre	les nôtres	les nôtres
yours	le vôtre	la vôtre	les vôtres	les vôtres
theirs	le leur	la leur	les leurs	les leurs

Examples

C'est ton stylo. C'est le tien. = It's your pen. It's yours.
Est-ce que c'est le chien de Marie? Oui, c'est le sien. =
Is it Marie's dog? Yes, it's hers.
Est-ce que c'est la chemise de Paul? Oui, c'est la sienne. =
Is it Paul's shirt? Yes, it's his.

Exercise

Fill in the correct form of the *possessive pronoun* given in brackets.

a) Voilà des livres. Ce sont . . . (mine)
b) Voilà un chandail. C'est . . . (hers)
c) Voilà des clefs. Ce sont . . . (ours)
d) Voilà un gant. C'est . . . (yours)
e) Voilà une voiture blanche. C'est . . . (theirs)

27) This, that, these, those

a) Use the following forms when *this, that, these, those* are *adjectives*.

	singular	*plural*
masculine	ce	ces
feminine	cette	ces

Ce has an alternative form, cet, for masculine singular words that begin with a vowel or h. Feminine singular words that begin with a vowel or h use the normal feminine singular form.

Examples

Ce livre est neuf. = **This** book is new.
Ces livres sont vieux. = **These** books are old.
Cette jeune fille est jolie. = **That** girl is pretty.
Cet œuf n'est pas bon. = **This** egg is not good.

To show the difference between *this* and *that*, add -ci to the noun for *this*, and add -là to the noun for *that*.

Examples

Ce stylo-ci est le mien, ce stylo-là est le tien. = **This** pen is mine, **that** pen is yours.
Cet homme-ci est mon père, cet homme-là est mon oncle. = **This** man is my father, **that** man is my uncle.

Exercise

Put in ce, cette, cet, or ces.

a) . . . homme est mon grand-père.
b) Je n'aime pas . . . poire.
c) Elle va achcter . . . chaussures,
d) Nous ne parlons pas à . . . garçon.
e) . . . œufs ne sont pas frais.

b) Use the following forms when *this one, that one, these, those* are *pronouns* — when the noun is not mentioned.

	singular	*plural*
masculine	celui	ceux
feminine	celle	celles

Although the noun is not mentioned in the same sentence as celui, etc., it must have been mentioned earlier on, so that you know which of the above forms to use. To show the difference between *this one* and *that one*, add -ci for *this one* or *these*, and add -là for *that one* or *those*.

Examples

a) Quelle est ta **maison?** Celle-là. = Which is your **house?** That one.
b) De quel **garçon** parles-tu? De **celui** qui est près de la porte. = Which **boy** are you talking about? That one (the one) who is near the door.
c) Tu n'as pas de **pantoufles?** Prends celles-ci. = You haven't any **slippers?** Take these.

Exercise

Fill in **celui-ci (-là), celle-ci (-là), ceux-ci (-là),** or **celles-ci (-là).**

a) Choisissez une robe. Je voudrais . . .
b) Veux-tu des gâteaux? Oui, je prends . . .
c) Cette règle est la mienne, . . . est la sienne.
d) Je voudrais des chaussures. Puis-je essayer . . .?
e) Quel est ton manteau? . . . .

28) Tout – all, every, the whole, everything

	singular	*plural*
masculine	tout	tous
feminine	toute	toutes

Used just like any other adjective, **tout** etc., mean *all, the whole* and *every*. **Le, la, les** are normally needed except when they are replaced by possessive adjectives.

Examples

J'ai perdu **tous** mes livres. = I have lost **all** my books.
J'ai travaillé **toute** la journée. = I have worked **all** day.
(I have worked **the whole** day)
Je viens ici **tous** les jours. = I come here **every** day.

Tout meaning *everything* does not change:

Il m'a **tout** laissé. = He has left me **everything.**
Nous partageons **tout.** = We share **everything.**

Tous, toutes meaning *all* when standing alone, do not need **le, la, les:**

Ils sont **tous** là.
Elles sont **toutes** là. } = They are all there.

Special Phrases:

Tout le monde. = Everyone, everybody.
Tous les deux. = Both.

Exercise

Fill in **tout, toute, tous,** or **toutes.**

a) Il a fini . . . les gâteaux.
b) . . . les jeunes filles jouent au netball.
c) Ecoutez, . . . le monde.
d) Nous invitons . . . nos voisins.
e) . . . la maison est froide.

29) Comparison of adjectives – bigger, more intelligent, etc.

young	= jeune		difficult	= difficile
younger	= **plus** jeune		more difficult	= **plus** difficile
youngest =	{ **le (la) plus** jeune		most difficult =	{ **le (la) plus** difficile
	les plus jeunes			**les plus** difficiles

From the above examples, you can see that:

a) **Plus** = *more* . . . or *er* at the end of the adjective.
b) **Le (la, les) plus** = *most* . . . or *est* at the end of the adjective.

Remember that the adjective must still match the noun it describes.

Examples

a) Elle est **plus** petite que moi. = She is **smaller** than me.
Il est **plus** intelligent que Marcel. = He is **more** intelligent than Marcel.
b) Ce sont **les plus** grands magasins de la ville. = They are he biggest shops in town.
c) Je lis le livre **le plus** intéressant de la bibliothèque. = I am reading the **most** interesting book in the library.

Note that **que** means *than*, and **de** means *in* with these examples.
If the adjective normally follows the noun it describes, then **le (la** or **les) plus** must be placed after the noun:

> La jeune fille **paresseuse.** = The lazy girl.
> La jeune fille **la plus paresseuse.** = The laziest girl.

Use **moins** to mean *less*:

> Elle est **moins** grande que toi. = She is **less** tall than you.
> Nous sommes **moins** riches que vous. = We are **less** rich than you.

Use **aussi . . . que** to mean *as . . . as*:

> Vous êtes **aussi** stupide **qu'eux.** = You are as stupid as them.
> Il est **aussi** vieux **que** lui. = He is as old as him.

However, after ne . . . pas use si instead of aussi:

> Tu **n'es pas si** grand **que** moi. = You are **not** as big as me.

Special point

Some adjectives have special forms, such as:

bon = good	**meilleur** = better	**le meilleur** = best
mauvais = bad	**pire** = worse	**le pire** = worst

Exercise

Fill in **le (la, les) plus, moins,** or **aussi** + the adjective in brackets.
Choose the form which makes most sense.

a) Il est . . . que moi. (jeune)
b) Nous sommes . . . qu'eux. (méchant)
c) Elle porte une . . . jupe que Sophie. (long)
d) J'ai . . . voiture du village. (grand)
e) Ce livre-ci est . . . que celui-là. (bon)

30) Adverbs

a) *Formation of adverbs*
Many adverbs in English end in *ly* and many in French end in **ment**.
If an adjective ends in a *vowel*, you can form the adverb by adding
ment to the masculine singular form of the adjective. If an adjective
ends in a *consonant*, form the adverb by adding **ment** to the feminine
singular form of the adjective.

Examples

rare = rare	rarement = rarely
vrai = real	vraiment = really
doux = sweet	*feminine singular form* = douce doucement = sweetly
heureux = happy	*feminine singular form* = heureuse heureusement = happily

Exercise

Make these adjectives into adverbs.

a) complet b) cruel c) franc d) joli e) dangereux

b) *Comparison of adverbs*
Adverbs can be compared in the same way as adjectives. (See Chapter 29)

> quickly = **vite**/more quickly = **plus vite**/most quickly = **le plus vite**
> (always **le**)

Other examples

> Il court **aussi** vite **que** moi. = He runs **as** quickly as me.
> Elle joue **moins** heureusement que son frère. = She plays **less** happily than her brother.

Special point

Some adverbs have irregular forms, such as:

bien = well	mieux = better	le mieux = best
beaucoup = much	plus ⁻ more	le plus = most
peu = a little	moins = less	le moins = least
mal = badly	pire = worse	le pire = worst

Exercise

Fill in **(le) plus, moins, aussi,** plus the adverb in brackets. Choose the form which makes most sense.

   a) Nous lisons . . . que Michel. (vite)
   b) Elle danse . . . que moi. (bien)
   c) J'écris . . . que ma sœur. (lentement)
   d) Il travaille . . . le soir. (heureusement)

31) Future tense – I shall eat, he will stay, etc.

The future tense shows what *will* happen, tomorrow, next month, or at some time in the future. All verbs, regular and irregular, have the same endings for the future tense.

a) *Er, ir, re verbs*
To form the future tense, the endings given below should be added to the *infinitive*. (See *Explanation of English Terms Used.*) An re infinitive drops the final e before the endings. Irregular verbs may not all use the infinitive to form this tense. Check the verb tables first. (See Chapter 58.)

je has ending **ai**	**nous** has ending **ons**
tu has ending **as**	**vous** has ending **ez**
il has ending **a**	**ils** has ending **ont**
elle has ending **a**	**elles** has ending **ont**

Examples

a) I shall give ⟶ add ending ai to infinitive **donner**.
Final answer: **Je donnerai.**
b) We shall choose ⟶ add ending ons to infinitive **choisir**.
Final answer: **Nous choisirons.**
c) You (s) will sell ⟶ add ending as to infinitive **vendre**, but remember to drop the final e of **vendre**.
Final answer: **Tu vendras.**

Exercise

Put the verbs in **bold** print into the future tense.

a) Elle **finit** ses devoirs.
b) Vous **rentrez** à la maison.
c) Ils **attendent** l'autobus.
d) Je **joue** au tennis.
e) Le matin, nous **entendons** les oiseaux.

b) *Etre and avoir, and reflexive verbs*
Etre and **avoir** have irregular stems in the future tense:

Etre = To Be   Avoir = To Have

je serai	nous serons	j'aurai	nous aurons
tu seras	vous serez	tu auras	vous aurez

| il sera | ils seront | il aura | ils auront |
| elle sera | elles seront | elle aura | elles auront |

Reflexive verbs have the same endings as other verbs and are formed in the same way. (See Chapter 31a). Remember to add the correct reflexive pronoun.

Examples

a) I shall get up ⟶ add ending ai to infinitive **lever**.
Remember to add reflexive pronoun me.
Final answer: **Je me lèverai.**
b) He will shave ⟶ add ending a to infinitive **raser**.
Remember to add reflexive pronoun se.
Final answer: **Il se rasera.**

Exercise

Put the verbs in **bold** print into the future tense.

a) Nous **sommes** à l'école.
b) Il **a** de l'argent.
c) Tu te **reposes** le soir.
d) Vous **avez** des vêtements neufs.
e) Michel et Paul **sont** chez des amis.

32) Talking about the future using aller + infinitive

An immediate future can be formed using **aller** = to go as the main verb. (For **aller** see Chapter 58.) This gives the idea of *going to do* in English. The correct part of **aller** is used to match the subject of the sentence. The second verb always remains in the infinitive.

Examples

Je vais finir mes devoirs.
I am going to finish my homework.
Il va laver la voiture.
He is going to wash the car.
Nous allons attendre nos amis.
We are going to wait for our friends.

Exercise

Put the verbs in **bold** print into the future using **aller** + Infinitive.

a) Nous **rencontrons** notre ami.
b) Michel **vend** ses timbres.
c) Je me **repose.**
d) Est-ce que tu **rends** l'argent à Paul?
e) Les garçons **finissent** leur jeu.

33) Y, en

Y = there

Y can be used to make neater sentences instead of repeating a *place* already mentioned. **Y** must be placed immediately before the verb.

Examples

a) Nous allons **en ville.** Vous **y** allez aussi? = We are going into **town.** Are you going **there** too?
b) Est-ce qu'il travaille **à la banque?** Oui, il **y** travaille. = Does he work **at the bank?** Yes, he works there.

En = some, any

En can be used instead of repeating nouns that have **du, de la, de l',** or **des** in front of them.

Examples

a) Est-ce que vous avez **du thé?** Oui, j'**en** ai. = Have you **any tea?** Yes, I have (some).
b) Manges-tu **des bonbons?** Non, je n'**en** mange pas. = Are you eating **some sweets?** No, I'm not (eating any).
c) Est-ce qu'il y a **du beurre?** Oui, il y **en** a. = Is there **any butter?** Yes, there is (some).

En can also be used with quantities, again to avoid repetition. This time **en** has the idea *of it*, or *of them.*

Examples

a) Combien **de chats** a-t-il? Il **en** a deux. = How many **cats** has he? He has two (of them).

b) Elle a de **bons œufs.** J'en achète dix. = She has good **eggs.** I'm buying ten **(of them).**

c) Vous avez **du fromage?** J'en voudrais cent grammes. = Have you any **cheese?** I would like a hundred grams **(of it).**

See Chapter 34 for word order when using **y** and **en.**

Exercise

Replace the words in **bold** print with **y** or **en.** Choose whichever makes most sense.

a) Est-ce que le professeur va souvent **en France?**
b) Il porte deux **sacs.**
c) Nous achetons **du sucre.**
d) Vous allez **dans la cour** à midi.
e) J'ai trois **frères.**

34) Object pronouns – me, you, him, her, etc.

direct object		*indirect object*	
me	= me	**me**	= to me
te	= you	**te**	= to you
le	= him, it	**lui**	= to him, to her, to it
la	= her, it	**nous**	= to us
nous	= us	**vous**	= to you
vous	= you	**leur**	= to them
les	= them		

Think of these English sentences:

a) I saw *him* later.   a) He met *her* today. a) We watched *them*
b) I spoke to *him* later. b) He wrote to *her*.   b) We sang to *them.*

In English, object pronouns are placed after the verb, while in French, they are placed immediately *before* the verb. In the **a)** sentences above, *him*, *her*, and *them* are called direct object pronouns. In the **b)** sentences above, the word *to* comes before the pronouns, so these are called indirect object pronouns. It is important to be able to tell which pronouns are direct and which indirect, when you use the perfect tense in French. (See *Explanation of English Terms Used* and Chapter 38)

In French, there are different pronouns for *him* (**le**), *to him* (**lui**), *her* (**la**), *to her* (**lui**), *them* (**les**), *to them* (**leur**). The rest of the pronouns have the same form whether direct or indirect.

Examples

She likes **us**. = Elle **nous** aime.
She is talking **to us**. = Elle **nous** parle.
We are chasing **them**. = Nous **les** chassons.
We write **to them** often. = Nous **leur** écrivons souvent.

Exercise

Replace the words in **bold** print with the correct object pronoun.

a) Nous cherchons **le café**.
b) Elle parle **à son professeur**.
c) Vous achetez **les bananes**.
d) Je lave **la voiture**.

Word Order
If there are two pronouns in a sentence, the following word order
should be used:

me	le				
te	la	lui	y	en ⟶	*verb*
nous	les	leur			
vous					

That is, **en** is placed nearest the verb, and **me** is placed furthest away.

Examples

Il **nous les** donne. = He gives **them to us**.
Vous **le lui** passez. = You are passing **it to him**.

35) Commands and object pronouns

In a command, the object pronouns *follow* the verb (as in English),
if the command is *to do* something. The pronouns go before the
verb (as normal) if the command is *not to do* something.

Examples

Ecrivez-**nous**. = Write **to us**.
Ne **nous** écrivez pas. = Don't write **to us**.

Racontez-**le-lui**. = Tell **him** it.
Ne **le lui** racontez pas. = Don't tell **him** it.

Special points

a) Use **moi** instead of **me**, when the command is to do something.
Me is used as normal when the command is not to do something:

Dis-**moi**. = Tell **me**.
Ne **me** dis pas. = Don't tell **me**.

b) When the command is to do something, the following word order
should be used.

verb	le la les	moi toi lui nous vous leur	y	en

Exceptions to this are **moi** and **toi** become **me** and **te** before **y** & **en**.

Donne-**les-moi**. = Give them **to me**.
Montrez-**nous-en**. = Show **us some**.
Passe-**m'en**. = Pass **me some**.

Exercise

Change the words in **bold** print into object pronouns.

a) Montrez **les chaussures à mon amie**.
b) Ne donne pas **le livre aux enfants**.
c) Cherche **les jeunes filles**.
d) Ne passez pas **la viande à Paulette**.

36) Strong pronouns – moi, toi, etc.

moi	= me	**nous**	= us	
toi	= you	**vous**	= you	
lui	= him	**eux**	= them (m)	
elle	= her	**elles**	= them (f)	
soi	= oneself			

Strong pronouns are not the same as object pronouns, and should only be used in certain cases. The most common uses are:

i) With **C'est** or **Ce sont**:
   C'est **nous** = It's **us**.   Ce sont **eux.** = It's **them.**
ii) For emphasis, without any meaning of its own:
   Moi, je ne l'aime pas. = **I** don't like him.
   Toi, tu ne viens pas. = **You're** not coming.
iii) With **même** meaning self:
   moi-même = myself.   elles-mêmes = themselves.
iv) On its own, after a question:
   Qui a fini? **Moi.**
   Who has finished? **Me.**
v) With prepositions:
   avec **nous** = with **us**   après **vous** = after **you**
vi) Comparing one person to another:
   Elles sont plus jolies qu'**elle.**
   They are prettier than **her.**
   Nous sommes plus intelligents que **toi.**
   We are more intelligent than **you.**

Special point

Soi generally meaning *oneself* can mean *himself* but should only be used with **on** = one, **chacun** = each one, **personne** = nobody, or **tout le monde** = everyone:

Tout le monde travaille pour soi.
Everyone works for **himself.**

Exercise

Fill in any *strong pronoun* that makes sense, and then put the sentences into English.

a) Qui est-ce? C'est . . .
b) Nous sommes plus aimables que . . .
c) Je vais au cinéma avec . . .
d) Elle marche plus vite que . . .
e) Tu y vas sans . . .

37) **Perfect (past) tense – I have seen, I saw, etc.**

The perfect (past) tense shows what *has* happened, or what happened yesterday, last week, or at some time in the past. The perfect tense is usually formed using the verb avoir in the present tense, along with the past participle of the second verb.

To form the past participle of er verbs, add é to the stem:

lancer = to throw   lancé = thrown
travailler = to work   travaillé = worked

To form the past participle of ir verbs, add i to the stem:

remplir = to fill   rempli = filled
choisir = to choose   choisi = chosen

To form the past participle of re verbs, add u to the stem:

vendre = to sell   vendu = sold
attendre = to wait   attendu = waited

There are many irregular past participles which should be learned by heart. The most common will be found in the verb tables. (See Chapter 58). Check the past participle before trying to form the perfect tense of any verb.

Examples

a) **We have worked**⟶we = nous + correct part of **avoir** — **nous avons**. + Travailler = to work⟶past participle = **travaillé**.
Final answer: **Nous avons travaillé.**
b) **She has finished**⟶she = elle + correct part of **avoir** — **elle a.** + Finir = to finish⟶past participle = **fini**.
Final answer: **Elle a fini.**

Confusion can arise because the perfect tense in French can have two meanings in English. For example, **J'ai mangé** can mean **I have eaten** or **I ate**, depending on the sentence.

J'ai déjà mangé ce matin. = I have already eaten this morning.
J'ai mangé hier. = I ate yesterday.

Example of perfect tense for reference

J'ai donné = I have given *or* I gave
tu **as donné** = you (s) have given *or* you (s) gave
il **a donné** = he/it has given *or* he/it gave
elle **a donné** = she/it has given *or* she/it gave
nous **avons donné** = we have given *or* we gave
vous **avez donné** = you (pl) have given *or* you (pl) gave
ils **ont donné** = they (m) have given *or* they (m) gave
elles **ont donné** = they (f) have given *or* they (f) gave

Exercise

Put the verbs in **bold** print into the perfect tense. Check past participles first.

a) Alain **choisit** un disque.
b) Tu **manges** trop!
c) J'**attends** un train.
d) Il **achète** un chien.
e) Nous **voyons** un grand bateau.

Special points

Etre and avoir follow the above rules for the perfect tense, but they have irregular past participles, which are:

être = to be   past participle = été
avoir = to have   past participle = eu

Examples

Il **a eu** un accident. = He **has had** an accident.
Nous **avons été** chez Guy. = We **have been** at Guy's.

(For reflexive verbs in the perfect tense — see Chapter 39.)

38) Perfect tense agreement with object pronouns

If a *direct object pronoun* is placed before the avoir part of a verb in the perfect tense, the past participle must match (or agree with) the object pronoun, as if it was an adjective. (For object pronouns — see Chapter 34.)

Examples

a) I have lost my shirt.   I have lost it.
J'ai perdu ma chemise.   Je l'ai perdue.

In this example, l' stands for the feminine singular **chemise**. L' is placed before the verb, so the past participle **perdu** must match l'. To make the past participle feminine singular, you must add e, just as you would with any other adjective.

b) She has eaten **the chocolates.**   She has eaten **them.**
Elle a mangé **les chocolats.**   Elle **les** a mangés.

In the above example, **les** stands for the masculine plural **chocolats. Les** is placed before the verb, so the past participle **mangé**
must match **les**. To make the past participle masculine and plural,
you must add s, just as you would with any other adjective.

N.B. The past participle never matches an indirect object.

Special point

Agreement may occur when the direct object is a noun, if the form
of the sentence means that the direct object is placed before the
whole verb.

Examples

a) Combien de **pommes** as-tu achetées? = How many apples did
you buy?
Achetées matches the feminine plural **pommes** in this case, only
because the question form of the sentence has placed **pommes**
before the verb.
b) Voici **la robe que** j'ai choisie. = Here's the dress that I bought.
Que meaning *that* refers to the feminine singular **la robe**. Both
come before the verb and so **choisie** matches **la robe**.

Exercise

Change the words in **bold** print into object pronouns and make the
past participle match the pronoun *if necessary.*

a) J'ai envoyé **les fleurs** à maman.
b) Elle a passé **le café** à Pierre.
c) Nous avons acheté **cette voiture noire.**
d) Ils ont invité **Claudine.**

39) Verbs using être with the perfect tense

a) All reflexive verbs use être instead of avoir when forming the
perfect tense. The past participle agrees with (matches) the reflexive
pronoun (See Chapter 18), which in turn agrees with the subject of
the sentence. So, in all but two cases, you can think of the past
participle as matching the subject. The exceptions are:

i) When there is a direct object, no agreement takes place:
Elle s'est lavé les mains. = She has washed her hands.
Les mains is the direct object.
Nous nous sommes brossé **les dents.** = We have brushed
our teeth. **Les dents** is the direct object.
ii) When the reflexive pronoun becomes the indirect object —
to me, to one another, etc., no agreement takes place:

Elles se sont écrit. = They wrote to each other.
Vous **vous** êtes téléphoné. = You telephoned each other.

The following examples show the usual rule for agreement:

Tu t'es promenée, **Claudine?** = Have you been for a walk,
Claudine?
Les enfants se sont couchés. = The children have gone to bed.

b) There are 16 common verbs which also use **être** to form the
perfect tense, and the past participle always matches the subject.
These verbs are:

arriver = to arrive	**aller** = to go
partir = to leave	**venir** = to come
entrer = to enter	**rester** = to stay
sortir = to go out	**revenir** = to come back
retourner = to return	**monter** = to go up
rentrer = to return/go home	**descendre** = to go down
naître = to be born	**tomber** = to fall
mourir = to die	**devenir** = to become

Examples

Nous sommes allés au bord de la mer. = We went to the seaside.
Marie et Claudine sont entrées dans un café. = Marie and Claudine
went into a café.

Special point

The verbs **monter** and **descendre** may use **avoir** as usual, *provided
they are followed by a direct object:*

Ils ont descendu **la pente** très vite. = They went down the slope
very quickly.

Monter and **descendre** often mean *to take/carry/bring up* and *to take/carry/bring down* when using avoir. For example:
J'ai **monté** les valises = I have **taken up** the cases.

Exercise

Change the verbs in **bold** print into the perfect tense using être.

a) Nous **entrons** dans la salle de classe.
b) Les dames **arrivent** à la gare.
c) Il **tombe** dans le jardin.
d) Pauline **se réveille** de bonne heure.
e) Je **me lave.**

40) Venir de and depuis

These two constructions have meanings in English in the past tense, but use the present or imperfect (See Chapter 41) tenses in French, *never* the perfect tense.

Venir de = To have just (done something) — using the present tense. The second verb must always be in the *infinitive.*

Examples

Il **vient d'arriver.** = He **has just** arrived.
Nous **venons de** téléphoner. = We **have just** telephoned.

Depuis = Since, for — in time phrases showing a continued action. Again use the present tense.

Examples

J'**étudie** le français **depuis** deux ans. = I **have been studying** French **for** two years.
Ils **cherchent** une maison **depuis** octobre. = They **have been looking** for a house **since** October.

Exercise

Answer the following questions, putting in the correct form of the verb to match the subject. For example:

Je viens de finir. Et Marc?
Answer: Marc **vient** de finir.

a) Elle vient de trouver de l'argent. Et les garçons?
b) Nous venons de manger. Et toi?
c) Ils viennent de se laver. Et vous?
d) Tu habites ici depuis un mois. Et Pierre?
e) Je joue au tennis depuis une heure. Et les jeunes filles?

41) Imperfect tense – I was going, I used to go, etc.

The imperfect tense shows what someone *was doing*, or what someone *used to do*, or what *was happening* in the past.

a) *Er, ir, re verbs*
The same endings are used for all verbs and should be added to the *stem* of the **nous** form of the present tense.

je has ending ais	nous has ending ions
tu has ending ais	vous has ending iez
il has ending ait	ils has ending aient
elle has ending ait	elles has ending aient

Examples

a) **You (s) were singing** ⟶ add ending **ais** to the stem of chanter (**chant**).
Final answer: **Tu chantais.**
b) **They used to wait** ⟶ add ending **aient** to the stem of attendre (**attend**).
Final answer: **Ils attendaient.**

Exercise

Put the verbs in **bold** print into the imperfect tense.

a) Claudine **demande** l'heure.
b) Je **remplis** des boîtes.
c) Vous **appelez** un ami.
d) Paul et Michel **marchent** dans le parc.
e) Nous **descendons** à la cuisine.

b) *Etre and avoir, and reflexive verbs*
The imperfect tense of **être** is irregular, but **avoir** follows the usual pattern.

Etre = To Be

j'étais	nous étions
tu étais	vous étiez
il était	ils étaient
elle était	elles étaient

Reflexive verbs have the same endings as other verbs, but you must remember to add the reflexive pronoun.

Examples

a) **We used to go for a walk** ——→add ending **ions** to the stem of promener (promen). Remember to add the reflexive pronoun nous.
Final answer: **Nous nous promenions.**
b) **She was brushing** her teeth——→add ending **ait** to the stem of **brosser (bross)**. Remember to add the reflexive pronoun **se**.
Final answer: **Elle se brossait** les dents.

Exercise

Put the verbs in **bold** print into the imperfect tense.

a) Je **suis** dans le jardin.
b) Nous **avons** un chien.
c) Tu **te peignes.**
d) Nicole **a** deux poupées.
e) Les enfants **se dépêchent** à l'école.

Special point

The imperfect tense is used with **venir de** and **depuis** (See Chapter 40) instead of the pluperfect tense. (See Chapter 42.) For example:

Il **venait de** partir, quand son père est arrivé. = He **had just** left, when his father arrived.
Elle **apprenait** l'allemand **depuis** trois ans, quand elle est allée habiter en Allemagne. = She **had been learning** German **for** three years when she went to live in Germany.

42) Pluperfect (past perfect) tense – I had bought, we had made, etc.

The pluperfect tense shows what *had* happened, or what someone *had* done in the past. The pluperfect tense is formed with the imperfect tense of avoir or être (See Chapters 39 and 41b) and the past participle. The same rules for past participle agreement apply as for the perfect tense. (See Chapters 38 and 39).

a) *Er, ir, re verbs*

Examples

a) **They had broken** ——➤ they had = ils **avaient** ——➤ add the past participle of **casser** (**cassé**).
Final answer: Ils avaient cassé.
b) **I had chosen** ——➤ I had = j'**avais** ——➤ add the past participle of **choisir** (**choisi**).
Final answer: **J'avais choisi.**
c) **He had come down** ——➤ he had = il **était** ——➤ add the past participle of **descendre** (**descendu**).
Final answer: Il était descendu.
d) **We had gone home** ——➤ we had = nous **étions** ——➤ add the past participle of **rentrer** (**rentré**).
Final answer: Nous étions rentrés. — Note that **rentrés** matches the plural subject **nous**.

Reference chart of pluperfect forms

J'étais arrivé(e) = I had arrived	J'avais fini = I had finished
tu étais arrivé(e)	tu avais fini
il était arrivé	il avait fini
elle était arrivée	elle avait fini
nous étions arrivés(es)	nous avions fini
vous étiez arrivé(s/e/es)	vous aviez fini
ils étaient arrivés	ils avaient fini
elles étaient arrivées	elles avaient fini

Exercise

Change the verbs in **bold** print into the pluperfect tense.

a) Nous **avons acheté** un électrophone.
b) Tu **as fait** la vaisselle.
c) Ils **ont mis** leur veste.
d) Elle **est retournée** de bonne heure.
e) Vous **êtes devenu** célèbre.

b) *Etre and avoir, and reflexive verbs*
Etre and **avoir** follow the same pattern as other verbs, but they have irregular past participles.

Etre = To Be   Avoir = To Have

J'avais été = I had been, etc.   J'avais eu = I had had, etc.

Reflexive verbs use the imperfect tense of être to form the pluperfect tense. Remember to add the reflexive pronoun before the part of être, and the past participle must match the reflexive pronoun. (See Chapter 39).

Examples

a) **She had combed her hair** ⟶ she had = elle était ⟶ add the past participle of **peigner (peigné)**. Remember to add the reflexive pronoun s' and that **peigné** must match the reflexive pronoun s' which is standing for **elle**.
Final answer: **Elle s'était peignée.**
b) **We had washed** ⟶ we had = nous étions ⟶ add the past participle of **laver (lavé)**. Remember to add the reflexive pronoun **nous** and that **lavé** must match the reflexive pronoun **nous** which is standing for the subject **nous**.
Final answer: **Nous nous étions lavés.**

Exercise

Change the verbs in **bold** print into the pluperfect tense.

a) Michel **a eu** trop de gâteaux.
b) Elle **a été** malade.
c) Vous vous **êtes trompé**.
d) Je me **suis couché** tard.
e) Nous **avons eu** beaucoup de lettres.

43) Conditional tense – I should like, he would find, etc.

The conditional tense shows what *should or would* happen, or what someone *should or would* do. All verbs have the same endings for the conditional tense, and these are added to the infinitive in the same way that the future tense was formed. (See Chapter 31). The endings are in fact the same as those used for the imperfect tense. (See Chapter 41).

a) *Er, ir, re verbs*

je has ending ais	nous has ending ions
tu has ending ais	vous has ending iez
il has ending ait	ils has ending aient
elle has ending ait	elles has ending aient

Examples

a) **You (pl) would like** ⟶ add ending **iez** to infinitive **aimer**.
Final answer: **Vous aimeriez.**
b) **I should choose** ⟶ add ending **ais** to infinitive **choisir**.
Final answer: **Je choisirais.**
c) **He would sell** ⟶ add ending **ait** to infinitive **vendre** (but remember to drop the final **e**). Final answer: **Il vendrait.**

Exercise

Change the verbs in **bold** print into the conditional tense.

a) Nous **choisissons.**
b) Ils **rendent** leurs livres.
c) Je n'**aime** pas travailler.
d) Tu **finis.**
e) Elle **rencontre.**

b) *Etre and avoir, and reflexive verbs*
Etre and **avoir** keep the irregular stems as used in the future tense.

Etre = To Be   **Avoir = To Have**

Je serais = I should be, etc.   **J'aurais** = I should have, etc.

Reflexive verbs follow the same pattern as other verbs, but remember to add the reflexive pronoun:

Je me réveillerais = I should wake up, etc.

Exercise

Change the verbs in **bold** print into the conditional tense.

a) Il **se lève** de bonne heure.
b) Nous **sommes** riches.
c) Elles **ont** beaucoup de disques.
d) Vous **êtes** fou.
e) Je **me promène.**

Special point

If you can replace *would* with *used to* in English, *without changing the meaning of the sentence*, then you must use the imperfect tense instead of the conditional.

Examples

a) He **would buy** a newspaper every evening. = He **used to buy** a newspaper every evening. = Il **achetait** un journal chaque soir.
b) She **would visit** her friend each summer. = She **used to visit** her friend each summer. = Elle **rendait** visite à son amie chaque été.

44) 'On' – someone, you, they, we, and one

On is a useful device in French that is very commonly used. It is now often used in spoken French instead of **nous** (we). The idea of the person is very vague, and **on** can be used for any one of the above meanings. Use the part of the verb that usually goes with il.

Examples

a) **On** a frappé à la porte. = **Someone** knocked at the door.
b) **On** va au cinéma ce soir. = **We** are going to the cinema this evening.
c) **On** achète les bonbons à la confiserie. = **You (one)** can buy sweets at the sweet shop.

Exercise

Fill in the correct part of the verb given in brackets. Write your answers in English, too.

a) On . . . le pain à la boulangerie. (acheter)
b) On . . . à la porte. (sonner)
c) On . . . écouter de la musique. (aller)
d) On . . . tous les jours. (manger)
e) On . . . dans la salle de bains. (se laver)

45) Quel, quelle, quels, quelles – what

These are used in questions or exclamations and act like any other
adjective.

	Singular	*Plural*
masculine	quel	quels
feminine	quelle	quelles

Examples

Quelle heure est-il? = **What** time is it?
Quel garçon! = **What** a boy!

Exercise

Fill in **quel, quelle, quels,** or **quelles.**

a) . . . est votre nom?
b) . . . livres?
c) . . . est ton adresse?
d) . . . robe!
e) . . . belles maisons!

46) Who and what in questions

a) *Who?*
Qui or **qui est-ce qui** = who as the subject of a question:

Qui est ton professeur? = **Who** is your teacher?
Qui est-ce qui le dit? = **Who** says so?

If there is already a subject (someone's name, or he, she, you, etc.),
you must use **qui** or **qui est-ce que** = who (object). If you use **qui,**
you must also use *inversion* of the verb. (See Chapter 20b):

Qui regardez-vous? = **Who (whom)** are you looking at?
Qui est-ce qu'il cherche? = **Who (whom)** is he looking for?

Use **qui** with prepositions such as à, de, avec, etc.:

Avec qui jouez-vous? = **Who** are you playing **with**?
De qui parle-t-elle? = **Who** is she talking **about**?

b) *What?*

Qu'est-ce qui = what as the subject of a question:

> **Qu'est-ce qui** vous fait mal? = **What** is hurting you?
> **Qu'est-ce qui** est tombé? = **What** has fallen?

If there is already a subject, use **que** or **qu'est-ce que** = what (object). If you use **que**, remember to use *inversion* of the verb:

> **Que** voulez-vous? = **What** do you want?
> **Qu'est-ce que** vous achetez? = **What** are you buying?

Use **quoi** with prepositions:

> Avec **quoi** est-ce que tu écris? = **What** are you writing with?
> A **quoi** pense-t-il? = **What** is he thinking about?

Exercise

Fill in **qui, qui est-ce qui, qui est-ce que, qu'est-ce qui, que, qu'est-ce que,** or **quoi.**

a) Avec . . . est-ce que vous dessinez?
b) . . . cherches-tu?
c) . . . il a trouvé?
d) A . . . est-ce qu'il parle?
e) De . . . avez-vous besoin?

47) Relative pronouns – who, whom, which, and that

Qui = who or which as the subject of a verb:

> La jeune fille **qui** porte la jupe verte. = The girl **who** is wearing the green skirt.
> La boîte **qui** est sur la table. = The box **which** is on the table.

Que (**qu'** before a vowel or h) = whom or which as the object of a verb:

> Le garçon **que** vous avez rencontré en ville. = The boy **whom** you met in town.
> Le chemisier **qu'**elle a choisi. = The blouse **which** she has chosen.

Note that, particularly in spoken English, the word *that* would probably be used for **qui** and **que.** Often, no word is used at all in spoken English when the relative pronoun is the object of a verb:

That is the girl I met yesterday. = That is the girl **whom** I met yesterday.

Use **qui** with prepositions such as **à, de, avec,** etc., when talking about *people*:

Voilà l'homme **à qui** je l'ai demandé. = There's the man (**whom**) I asked.
Tu connais le garçon **avec qui** elle sort. = You know the boy (**whom**) she's going out **with**.

Use **dont** to mean whose, of whom, of which:

J'ai téléphoné à l'homme **dont** j'ai trouvé le chien. = I telephoned the man **whose** dog I found.
Voilà le garçon **dont** j'ai parlé. = There's the boy **of whom** I spoke.

Special point

Dont is used instead of **qui** or **que** with verbs which must be followed by **de**. In such a case **de** disappears:

J'ai besoin de ce tissu. = I need that material.
Voici le tissu **dont** tu as besoin. = Here's the material **that** you need.

If **que** is used with the perfect tense, remember that it may be necessary to make the past participle match the word that **que** refers back to. (See Chapter 38). For example:

Voici les **chaussures que** j'ai achetées. = Here are the shoes **that** I bought.
Voici les **livres que** tu m'as prêtés. = Here are the books **that** you lent me.

If **qui** is used with the perfect tense using **être,** remember that it may be necessary to make the past participle match the word that **qui** refers back to, because verbs using **être** in the perfect tense must match their subject. (See Chapter 39). For example:

J'ai vu les **garçons qui** sont venus à la discothèque. = I saw the boys **who** came to the discotheque.
Voilà la **jeune fille qui** est tombée du train. = There's the girl **who** fell from the train.

Exercise

Fill in **qui, que,** or **dont.**

a) Regardez l'homme . . . parle.
b) Passez les lunettes . . . sont sur la table.
c) Voilà le garçon . . . la sœur s'est mariée.
d) Nous avons rencontré la dame . . . tu n'aimes pas.
e) C'était l'épicier à . . . j'ai téléphoné.

48) Lequel, laquelle, lesquels, lesquelles – which, that

Use the above forms with prepositions when talking about animals or things. They must match the word to which they refer.

Examples

a) Les **stylos** bleus **avec lesquels** j'écris toujours. = The blue pens **which** I always write **with.**
b) Les **salles dans lesquelles** ils se cachaient. = The rooms **which** they were hiding **in.**

Lequel etc., join with **à** and **de** to produce the following:

auquel	**duquel**
à laquelle	**de laquelle**
auxquels	**desquels**
auxquelles	**desquelles**

Examples

Le chat **auquel** l'enfant a donné de l'eau. = The cat **that** the child gave some water **to.**
Les bureaux **auxquels** j'ai écrit. = The offices **that** I wrote **to.**

When **lequel** etc., are relative pronouns, it is more common to use **dont** instead of the combined forms with **de** shown above. When **lequel** etc., are used in questions, the combined forms with **de** as shown above, *are* used, however. **Lequel** etc., are used in questions when offering a choice:

a) **Lequel** de ces livres voulez-vous? = **Which** of these books do you want?
b) **Laquelle** de ces jupes aimes-tu? = **Which** of these skirts do you like?

c) Elle a besoin d'un stylo. **Duquel?** = She needs a pen. **Which one?**

Exercise

Fill in **lequel, laquelle, lesquels, lesquelles** or a combined form with **à.**

a) Voilà le stylo sur . . . tu étais assis!
b) J'ai perdu les adresses . . . je dois écrire.
c) Donne-moi les crayons avec . . . tu dessinais.
d) Il a trouvé les jouets avec . . . l'enfant jouait.
e) . . . de ces gâteaux veux-tu?

49) Quand = when + the future tense

Consider this English sentence:

When I arrive, I shall have a bath.

The first part of the sentence is in the present tense, but this must be the future tense in French (when I shall arrive), in order to match the second part of the sentence:

a) Quand j'**arriverai**, je prendrai un bain. = When I **arrive**, I shall have a bath.
b) Quand il **sera** vieux, il sera chauve. = When he is old, he will be bald.

Exercise

Fill in the correct form of the verb given in brackets.

a) Quand je . . . je vous téléphonerai. (rentrer)
b) Quand il . . . nous irons le prendre. (arriver)
c) Quand nous . . . ils nous donneront du café. (entrer)
d) Quand tu . . . prêt, nous sortirons. (être)
e) Quand elles . . . je leur porterai du thé. (se réveiller)

50) Si = if + the present tense

The future tense must never be used in French with si, even if the meaning sometimes suggests a future time. Use the present tense as in English:

Si **elle vient**, nous irons au cinéma. = **If she comes**, we'll go to the cinema.
Si **nous gagnons**, nous achèterons une voiture. = **If we win**, we shall buy a car.

Exercise

Fill in the correct form of the verbs given in brackets.

a) Si tu . . . nous irons aux magasins. (vouloir)
b) Si elle . . . à temps, nous irons chez Pierre. (finir)
c) Si nous . . . tout, allons-y! (avoir)
d) Si je . . . bien, tu vas à l'étranger. (comprendre)
e) S'ils . . . vite, nous partirons bientôt. (s'habiller)

51) S'asseoir and être assis

The verb **s'asseoir** means to sit down and describes the action of someone in the process of sitting down. The verb **être assis** means to be seated or sitting, and describes the state of someone who has already sat down, and is therefore seated.

Examples

a) He is sitting in the car. This describes the state of being seated, so use **être assis**.
Il est assis dans la voiture.
b) She sat down quickly. This describes the action of sitting down, so use **s'asseoir**.
Elle s'est assise vite. Note the perfect tense.
c) We are going to sit down now. This describes the action of sitting down, so use **s'asseoir**.
Nous allons **nous asseoir** maintenant.

The present tense of s'asseoir is very irregular and should be learned by heart. (See Chapter 58) Etre assis follows the pattern of être, but assis is considered an adjective and so has to match the subject of the sentence. Note that the past participle of **s'asseoir** is also **assis**.

Exercise

Fill in the correct form of either s'asseoir or être assis.

a) Pierre . . . dans la salle à manger.
b) Nous . . . sur la plage.

c) Les garçons . . . maintenant.
d) . . . vite, les enfants!
e) Je . . . dans le salon.

52) The passive

The passive gives the idea of an action *being done to someone*
rather than *someone doing an action.* You will probably only need
to use the passive in compositions when describing situations and
actions.
   The passive is formed by using any tense of être with the past
participle of the main verb. The past participle then acts like an
adjective and must match the subject of the sentence.
   You will use the perfect and imperfect tenses most often in
French. Both tenses could be translated as *was* or *were* in English
and you must be careful to use the correct tense. The perfect tense
should be used if the action was done *once only.* The imperfect
tense should be used if the action was done *several times* or *over a
period of time.*

Examples

a) She **was injured** by a car.
The action happened only once, so use the perfect tense.
She **was** = she **has been** = elle a été ⟶ add the past participle
of **blesser (blessé).** Remember to make the past participle match
the subject.
Final answer: Elle a été blessée par une voiture.

b) The thief **was continually threatened** by the police.
The action happened often in the past, so use the imperfect
tense.
The thief **was** = le voleur était ⟶ add the past participle of
menacer (menacé). Remember to make the past participle match
the subject, if necessary.
Final answer: Le voleur était continuellement menacé par la
police.

Special point

You can avoid using the passive by using **on** instead, (See Chapter
44), as long as the person who has done the action is not mentioned.
She was injured could be turned into *someone injured her.* The vague
idea of *someone* is given by **on,** so the French becomes:

On l'a blessée. (blessée matches the object pronoun la, here l').

Exercise

Change the sentences into the passive.

a) On l'a attrapé.
b) On a fermé la porte.
c) On vend des glaces.
d) On montrait des robes.
e) On a tué le président.

53) Past historic tense

The past historic tense is used mainly in literary passages, and should not be used in conversation. You will probably only need to recognise this tense. The past historic is used for completed actions in the past, and for actions that happened over a period of time, if the whole period, in which the action took place, is seen as being in the past. For example:

The Second World War lasted six years.

Although the action continued over a period of time, the whole event happened in the past and so the past historic could be used.

The following verb endings are added to the *stem* of the verb used:

a) *Er verbs*

je has ending ai	nous has ending âmes
tu has ending as	vous has ending âtes
il has ending a	ils has ending èrent
elle has ending a	elles has ending èrent

b) *Ir verbs*

je has ending is	nous has ending îmes
tu has ending is	vous has ending îtes
il has ending it	ils has ending irent
elle has ending it	elles has ending irent

c) *Re verbs*

Most regular re verbs have the same endings as ir verbs, but some irregular ones like **connaître** = *to know*, or **lire** = *to read*, have the endings overleaf.

je has ending us	nous has ending ûmes
tu has ending us	vous has ending ûtes
il has ending ut	ils has ending urent
elle has ending ut	elles has ending urent

Examples

Ils réveillèrent papa de bonne heure et allèrent prendre le train de sept heures. = They woke father early and went to catch the seven o'clock train.
Elle visita beaucoup de pays il y a dix ans. = She visited many countries ten years ago.

d) *Etre and avoir, and reflexive verbs*

Reflexive verbs follow the same pattern as other verbs, but être and avoir have irregular *stems*, and use the alternative endings for re verbs.

Etre = To Be	Avoir = To Have
je fus = I was etc.	j'eus = I had etc.

Exercise

Put the following sentences into English.

a) Napoleon fut un célèbre empereur français.
b) Les enfants finirent de manger.
c) Nous entrâmes dans le café.
d) Il eut beaucoup à faire ce soir-là.
e) On s'amusa cette année-là.

54) Parts of the body – reference list

ankle	= la cheville	chin	= le menton	
arm	= le bras	ear	= une oreille	
back	= le dos	elbow	= le coude	
body	= le corps	eye	= un oeil	
cheek	= la joue	eyes	= les yeux	
chest	= la poitrine	face	{ = le visage	
			(= la figure	

finger	= le doigt	nail	= un ongle
foot	= le pied	neck	= le cou
forehead	= le front	nose	= le nez
hair	= les cheveux (m.pl.)	shoulder	= une épaule
hand	= la main	stomach	= l'estomac (m)
head	= la tête	tooth	= la dent
heel	= le talon	thigh	= la cuisse
hip	= la hanche	thumb	= le pouce
knee	= le genou	toe	= un orteil
leg	= la jambe	tongue	= la langue
lip	= la lèvre	waist	= la taille
mouth	= la bouche	wrist	= le poignet

Possessive adjectives are *not* used with parts of the body when a *reflexive* verb already shows possession or when an indirect object pronoun makes it clear whose bodily part is mentioned. (See Chapter 34).

Examples

Il **se lave les** mains. = He is washing **his** hands.
Ils **lui** ont cassé **la** jambe. = They broke his leg. (Without **lui** the sentence would mean that they each broke a leg.)

With + parts of the body is **au, à la, à l'**, or **aux**:

J'aime cette jeune fille **aux** cheveux bruns. = I like that girl with the brown hair.
Voilà l'homme **au** menton énorme! = There's the man with the huge chin!

55) Expressions with avoir – reference list

avoir x ans = to be x years old
avoir besoin de = to need
avoir chaud = to be warm, hot
avoir faim = to be hungry
avoir froid = to be cold
avoir lieu = to take place
avoir peur = to be afraid
avoir raison = to be right
avoir soif = to be thirsty
avoir tort = to be wrong

56) **Expressions with faire – reference list**

faire des achats = to do some shopping
faire attention = to pay attention, to be careful
faire du camping = to go camping
faire la connaissance de = to meet (for the first time)
faire la cuisine = to do the cooking
faire les devoirs = to do homework
faire la lessive = to do the washing
faire le ménage = to do the housework
faire des photos = to take some photos
faire une promenade = to go for a walk
faire une promenade en bateau = to go for a sail
faire une promenade en vélo = to go for a cycle ride
faire une promenade en voiture = to go for a drive
faire la vaisselle = to do the washing up

57) Slightly irregular 'er' verbs – reference list

The following common er verbs have spelling changes in certain tenses. Only the tenses with such changes are shown.

a) *Acheter = to buy*

Present

J'achète	nous achetons
tu achètes	vous achetez
il achète	ils achètent
elle achète	elles achètent

Conditional

J'achèterais, etc.

Future

J'achèterai	nous achèterons
tu achèteras	vous achèterez
il achètera	ils achèteront
elle achètera	elles achèteront

b) *Appeler = to call*

Present

J'appelle	nous appelons
tu appelles	vous appelez
il appelle	ils appellent
elle appelle	elles appellent

Conditional

J'appellerais, etc.

Future

J'appellerai	nous appellerons
tu appelleras	vous appellerez
il appellera	ils appelleront
elle appellera	elles appelleront

c) *Commencer = to begin*

Present

Je commence	nous commencns
tu commences	vous commencez
il commence	ils commencent
elle commence	elles commencent

Imperfect

Je commençais	nous commencions
tu commençais	vous commenciez
il commençait	ils commençaient
elle commençait	elles commençaient

c) Past historic

je commençai	nous commençâmes
tu commenças	vous commençâtes
il commença	ils commencèrent
elle commença	elles commencèrent

d) *Essayer = to try*

Present

		Future — The regular form keeping y may also be used.	
J'essaie	nous essayons	J'essaierai	nous essaierons
tu essaies	vous essayez	tu essaieras	vous essaierez
il essaie	ils essaient	il essaiera	ils essaieront
elle essaie	elles essaient	elle essaiera	elles essaieront

Conditional — The regular form keeping y may also be used.
J'essaierais, etc.

e) Lever = to raise (se lever = to get up)
   Same as *acheter = to buy*

f) *Manger = to eat*

Present

		Imperfect		*f) Past historic*	
Je mange	nous mangeons	Je mangeais	nous mangions	je mangeai	nous mangeâmes
tu manges	vous mangez	tu mangeais	vous mangiez	tu mangeas	vous mangeâtes
il mange	ils mangent	il mangeait	ils mangeaient	il mangea	ils mangèrent
elle mange	elles mangent	elle mangeait	elles mangeaient	elle mangea	elles mangèrent

g) *Nettoyer = to clean*
   Same as *essayer = to try* but there are no regular alternatives for the future and conditional tenses.

h) *Répéter = to repeat*

Present

Je répète	nous répétons
tu répètes	vous répétez
il répète	ils répètent
elle répète	elles répètent

You will meet other slightly irregular er verbs, but they will follow the pattern of the verbs given here.

58) Irregular verb tables

Infinitive	Command	Present	Future	Past participle	Past historic
aller to go	va allez allons	je vais, tu vas il/elle va nous allons vous allez ils/elles vont	j'irai	allé	j'allai
s'asseoir to sit down	assieds-toi asseyez-vous asseyons-nous	je m'assieds tu t'assieds il/elle s'assied nous nous asseyons vous vous asseyez ils s'asseyent elles s'asseyent	je m'assiérai	assis	j'assis
avoir to have	aie ayez ayons	j'ai, tu as il/elle a nous avons vous avez ils/elles ont	j'aurai	eu	j'eus
battre to beat	bats battons	je bats, tu bats il/elle bat nous battons vous battez ils/elles battent	je battrai	battu	je battis
boire to drink	bois buvez buvons	je bois, tu bois il/elle boit nous buvons vous buvez ils/elles boivent	je boirai	bu	je bus

Infinitive	Command	Present	Future	Past participle	Past historic
conduire to lead	conduis conduisez conduisons	je conduis tu conduis il/elle conduit nous conduisons vous conduisez ils conduisent elles conduisent	je conduirai	conduit	je conduisis
connaître to know	connais connaissez connaissons	je connais tu connais il/elle connaît nous connaissons vous connaissez ils connaissent elles connaissent	je connaîtrai	connu	je connus
courir to run	cours courez courons	je cours, tu cours il/elle court nous courons vous courez ils/elles courent	je courrai	couru	je courus
croire to believe	crois croyez croyons	je crois, tu crois il/elle croit nous croyons vous croyez ils/elles croient	je croirai	cru	je crus
devoir to owe to have to must	dois devez devons	je dois, tu dois il/elle doit nous devons vous devez ils/elles doivent	je devrai	dû (due)	je dus

Infinitive	Imperative	Present	Future	Past participle	Past historic
o say to tell	dites disons	il/elle dit nous disons vous dites ils/elles disent			
dormir to sleep	dors dormez dormons	je dors, tu dors il/elle dort nous dormons vous dormez ils/elles dorment	je dormirai	dormi	je dormis
écrire to write	écris écrivez écrivons	j'écris, tu écris il/elle écrit nous écrivons vous écrivez ils/elles écrivent	j'écrirai	écrit	j'écrivis
envoyer to send	envoie envoyez envoyons	j'envoie tu envoies il/elle envoie nous envoyons vous envoyez ils/elles envoient	j'enverrai	envoyé	j'envoyai
être to be	sois soyez soyons	je suis, tu es il/elle est nous sommes vous êtes ils/elles sont	je serai	été	je fus
faire to do to make	fais faites faisons	je fais, tu fais il/elle fait nous faisons vous faites ils/elles font	je ferai	fait	je fis
lire to read	lis lisez lisons	je lis, tu lis il/elle lit nous lisons vous lisez ils/elles lisent	je lirai	lu	je lus

Infinitive	Command	Present	Future	Past participle	Past historic
mettre to put	mets mettez mettons	je mets, tu mets il/elle met nous mettons vous mettez ils/elles mettent	je mettrai	mis	je mis
mourir to die	meurs mourez mourons	je meurs, tu meurs il/elle meurt nous mourons vous mourez ils/elles meurent	je mourrai	mort	je mourus
naître to be born	— —	il/elle naît ils/elles naissent	il/elle naîtra ils/elles naîtront	né	il/elle naquit ils/elles naquirent
offrir to offer	offre offrez offrons	j'offre, tu offres il/elle offre nous offrons vous offrez ils/elles offrent	j'offrirai	offert	j'offris
ouvrir to open	ouvre ouvrez ouvrons	j'ouvre, tu ouvres il/elle ouvre nous ouvrons vous ouvrez ils/elles ouvrent	j'ouvrirai	ouvert	j'ouvris
partir to leave	pars partez partons	je pars, tu pars il/elle part nous partons vous partez ils/elles partent	je partirai	parti	je partis
pouvoir to be able can	— — —	je peux (je puis) tu peux il/elle peut nous pouvons vous pouvez	je pourrai	pu	je pus

Infinitive	Imperative	Present	Future	Past participle	Past historic
prendre to take	prends prenez prenons	je prends tu prends il/elle prend nous prenons vous prenez ils/elles prennent	je prendrai	pris	je pris
recevoir to receive	reçois recevez recevons	je reçois tu reçois il/elle reçoit nous recevons vous recevez ils reçoivent elles reçoivent	je recevrai	reçu	je reçus
rire to laugh	ris riez rions	je ris, tu ris il/elle rit nous rions vous riez ils/elles rient	je rirai	ri	je ris
savoir to know	sache sachez sachons	je sais, tu sais il/elle sait nous savons vous savez ils/elles savent	je saurai	su	je sus
sentir to feel	sens sentez sentons	je sens, tu sens il/elle sent nous sentons vous sentez ils/elles sentent	je sentirai	senti	je sentis
servir to serve	sers servez servons	je sers, tu sers il/elle sert nous servons vous servez ils/elles servent	je servirai	servi	je servis

Infinitive	Command	Present	Future	Past participle	Past historic
sortir to go out to come out	sors sortez sortons	je sors, tu sors il/elle sort nous sortons vous sortez ils/elles sortent	je sortirai	sorti	je sortis
suivre to follow	suis suivez suivons	je suis, tu suis il/elle suit nous suivons vous suivez ils/elles suivent	je suivrai	suivi	je suivis
tenir to hold	tiens tenez tenons	je tiens tu tiens il/elle tient nous tenons vous tenez ils/elles tiennent	je tiendrai	tenu	je tins tu tins il/elle tint nous tînmes vous tîntes ils/elles tinrent
venir to come	viens venez venons	je viens tu viens il/elle vient nous venons vous venez ils/elles viennent	je viendrai	venu	je vins tu vins il/elle vint nous vînmes vous vîntes ils/elles vinrent
voir to see	vois voyez voyons	je vois, tu vois il/elle voit nous voyons vous voyez ils/elles voient	je verrai	vu	je vis
vouloir to want	veuille veuillez veuillons	je veux, tu veux il/elle veut nous voulons vous voulez ils/elles veulent	je voudrai	voulu	je voulus

59) Revision exercises

There are ten sentences for every five chapters. Read through the appropriate chapters before doing the exercises. To help you, the chapter number is shown at the end of each sentence.

Chapters 1 to 5 Fill in the spaces with any sensible answer.

a) Je veux acheter . . . chemise, et . . . chandail. (1)
b) Elle arrivera . . . matin. (5)
c) Il est né en . . . (5)
d) Il y a . . . enfants dans la classe. (3)
e) Nous ne trouvons pas . . . chat. (2)
f) Grand-mère visite le zoo chaque . . . (5)
g) Ii a beaucoup d'animaux. Il en a . . . (3)
h) Elle a acheté sa . . . voiture. (4)
i) Tu vas en vacances en . . . (5)
j) Maman va faire . . . jupe, et . . . robe pour Claudine. (1)

Chapters 6 to 10 Fill in the spaces according to the chapter numbers. There may be several correct answers to some of the sentences.

a) Nous quittons l'école à . . . (7)
b) Les mois d' . . . sont novembre, décembre, et janvier. (8)
c) Maman est . . . maison. (10)
d) La date de mon anniversaire est . . . (6)
e) Il fait chaud en . . . (8)
f) Nous allons . . . lac. (10)
g) Je prépare le dîner à . . . (7)
h) Elle va acheter . . . café, . . . lait, et . . . croissants. (9)
i) L'école commence . . . (6)
j) Au printemps, il . . . (8)

Chapters 11 to 15 Fill in the spaces according to the chapter numbers. Where a verb is to be used, it is given in brackets at the end of the sentence.

a) Voici les disques . . . Pierre. (11)
b) . . . le sel, s'il te plaît. (passer) (13)
c) Il . . . son ami. (attendre) (15)
d) . . . finissons les fruits. (12)
e) Elles . . . à l'agent. (répondre) (15)
f) . . . descends de ma chambre. (12)
g) Tu . . . des livres. (choisir) (14)

h) C'est la voiture ... professeur. (11)
i) ... le seau, Françoise. (remplir) (14)
j) ... du chocolat. (acheter) (13)

Chapters 16 to 20 Fill in the spaces according to the chapter numbers. Any verbs to be used are given in brackets at the end of the sentence. Turn the last three sentences into questions in two different ways.

a) Je ... dans la salle de bains. (être) (16)
b) Les garçons ... sous un arbre. (se reposer) (19)
c) Paulette et Claudine . : . des cadeaux. (avoir) (16)
d) Nous ... avons ... de sucre. (17)
e) Je ... lave tous les jours. (18)
f) Je ... vois ... (17)
g) Vous ... maintenant? (s'habiller) (19)
h) Il a trois chiens. (20)
i) Vous regardez un match de football. (20)
j) Elles attendent à l'arrêt d'autobus. (20)

Chapters 21 to 25 Fill in the spaces according to the chapter numbers. Adjectives to be used are given in brackets at the end of the sentence.

a) Paulette a une ... montre. (petit) (23)
b) Est-ce que tu habites ... Italie? (21)
c) Ils arriveront ... taxi. (22)
d) Il cherche ... chemise. (his) (25)
e) Je ne trouve pas ... cartable. (my) (25)
f) Papa porte une cravate ... (bleu) (23)
g) Il y a beaucoup de ... oranges. (beau) (24)
h) Il vient ... Marseille. (21)
i) Claudine a une jupe ... (neuf) (24)
j) Les enfants vont à la piscine ... vélo. (22)

Chapters 26 to 30 Fill in the spaces according to the chapter numbers.

a) Ce livre est ..., pas le tien. (26)
b) Il a mangé ... les fraises. (28)
c) Sa maison est ... grande de la ville. (29)
d) Cette jupe-ci est à Claudine, ... est à Monique. (27)
e) Ce sont les chaussures de Pierre. Ce sont ... (26)
f) Mon vélo est ... beau ... le tien. (29)
g) Je travaille ... les jours. (28)

h) Ces garçons-là sont sages, . . . sont méchants. (27)
i) Nous nageons bien, mais tu nages . . . (30)
j) Moi, je travaille peu, mais lui, il travaille . . . (30)

Chapters 31 to 35 Change the words in bold print into object pronouns, future tense, etc, according to the chapter numbers.

a) Vous travaillez **à la banque**. (33)
b) Il passe **les légumes à Maman**. (34)
c) Envoyons **cette lettre à nos amis**. (35)
d) J'ai deux frères. (33)
e) Nous **arrivons à six heures**. (31/32)
f) Claudine et Gisèle sont chez Hélène. (31)
g) Je voudrais un kilo **de pommes**. (33)
h) Pierre **t'attend** au coin de la rue. (31/32)
i) Prends **ces papiers**. (35)
j) Tu te **promènes** à la campagne. (31/32)

Chapters 36 to 40 Fill in the spaces according to the chapter numbers. Any verbs to be used are given in brackets at the end of the sentence.

a) Vous êtes partis sans . . . (36)
b) Nous . . . au cinéma hier soir. (aller) (39)
c) Marie . . . de beaux vêtements ce matin. (choisir) (37)
d) As-tu fini tes devoirs? Oui, je . . . finir mes devoirs. (40)
e) Ils . . . à notre école depuis un mois. (venir) (40)
f) C'est . . . qui va payer! (36)
g) J' . . . à Londres cette semaine. (être) (37)
h) André . . . de bonne heure, aujourd'hui. (se lever) (39)
i) Elle a acheté les journaux. Elle les a . . . (38)
j) Georges a vendu sa guitare. Il l'a . . . (38)

Chapters 41 to 45 Fill in the spaces according to the chapter numbers. Any verbs to be used are given in brackets at the end of the sentence.

a) Il . . . bien, quand il était jeune. (nager) (41)
b) J' . . . à Paris, si j'avais assez d'argent. (aller) (43)
c) On . . . les gâteaux à une pâtisserie. (vendre) (44)
d) . . . sorte de chocolats voulez-vous? (45)
e) Elle . . . tous les jours au marché. (aller) (41)
f) La leçon . . . quand il est arrivé. (commencer) (42)
g) . . . beau chat! (45)
h) On te . . . (chercher) (44)

i) Il . . . un vélo neuf pour son anniversaire. (vouloir) (43)
j) Ils . . . quand nous avons téléphoné. (partir) (42)

Chapters 46 to 51 Fill in the spaces according to the chapter
numbers. Any verbs to be used are given in brackets at the end of
the sentence.

a) Avec . . . est-ce que tu sors? (47)
b) Je chercherai ton pull quand je . . . (rentrer) (49)
c) Si la voiture . . ., nous partirons tout de suite. (marcher) (50)
d) Voici le nom du bureau . . . tu devrais écrire. (48)
e) . . . on va faire? (46)
f) Il m'a prêté le sac . . . il a acheté hier. (47)
g) . . . tout de suite, Georges! (51)
h) Nous voulons des chaussettes. . . .? (48)
i) . . . parle avec André? (46)
j) Les élèves . . . dans la salle de classe. (51)

Index

Numbers given refer to *chapter numbers*. French words are printed in **bold**.
Some terms may be explained further at the front of the book. (See *Explanation of English Terms Used*)